A Ring for the Millennium

A Guide to Wagner's *Der Ring des Nibelungen*

Peter Bassett has been listening to, and thinking and reading about, *The Ring* for more than thirty years, ever since hearing radio broadcasts of the Bayreuth Festival as a teenager. As a professional diplomat with academic training in politics and the law, Peter has been able to pursue his passion for opera—and Wagner's works in particular—in many of the famous opera houses of Europe. He is a member of the Board of Management of The State Opera of South Australia and the State Opera Ring Corporation, and is on the Committee of the Friends of The State Opera of South Australia and the Richard Wagner Society of South Australia.

This book was written to accompany the The State Opera of South Australia's 1998 Adelaide production of *The Ring*.

A Ring for the Millennium

A Guide to Wagner's *Der Ring des Nibelungen*

Peter Bassett

Wakefield Press

Wakefield Press
Box 2266
Kent Town
South Australia 5071

First published 1998

Copyright © Peter Bassett 1998

All rights reserved. This book is copyright. Apart from any fair dealing for the purposes of private study, research, criticism or review, as permitted under the Copyright Act, no part may be reproduced without written permission. Enquiries should be addressed to the publisher.

Design and typesetting by Michael Deves, Adelaide
Printed and bound by Hyde Park Press, Adelaide

Cover illustration: *Das Rheingold* by Peter Bassett
Title page illustration: gilt silver Viking ring, first millennium AD
(Statens Historiska Museum, Stockholm)

National Library of Australia
Cataloguing-in-Publication entry

Bassett, Peter.
A ring for the millennium: a guide to Wagner's Der Ring des Nibelungen.
ISBN 1 86254 471 9

1. Wagner, Richard, 1813–1883. Ring des Nibelungen. I. Title.

782.1

For my parents

and for Carol and Simon

Contents

Foreword ix
Preface x

An Introduction to *Der Ring des Nibelungen* 1

Synopsis 12

Das Rheingold 19

Die Walküre 35

Siegfried 63

Götterdämmerung 93

Notes 123
Significant dates 124
Further reading 128
Index 129

Fourteenth-century illumination showing Siegfried slaying the dragon

Foreword

Richard Wagner's *Der Ring des Nibelungen* is one of the great artistic achievements of Western civilisation. It is a massive work, and a great challenge to mount. The State Opera of South Australia is very pleased to be hosting the 1998 Adelaide production of *The Ring*, the first in Australia for 85 years and the first to be staged by an Australian team.

However, I am cognisant of the challenges that a production of *The Ring* also brings for audiences. With this in mind I invited Peter Bassett to give a series of pre-performance talks to guide *Ring*-goers through the lengthy cycle of four operas. Peter is a devoted Wagner scholar and a loyal supporter of both State Opera and the Wagner Society, and I can think of no-one more able to fulfil such a charge.

I am delighted with the lectures that Peter has prepared, and which he will give before each opera as the three cycles are presented in full in Adelaide in November. I am also pleased to learn that Peter has decided to publish a book based on his talks. This not only gives the lectures more permanence, but allows for some additional material that would not be suitable in the shorter format of a lecture to be included. It also makes Peter's lectures available to a wider audience.

It is with pleasure that I commend this book to lovers of Wagner's masterwork as part of the official program of State Opera's 1998 production of *Der Ring des Nibelungen*.

Stephen Phillips
MANAGING DIRECTOR • STATE OPERA RING CORPORATION
GENERAL DIRECTOR • THE STATE OPERA OF SOUTH AUSTRALIA

Preface

Richard Wagner might well have achieved fame and fortune earlier in life if he had chosen the path of writing popular *bel canto* operas in the style of Bellini and Donizetti, or romantic spectacles in the style of Meyerbeer and Halévy. That he could have done either was never in doubt. In Paris in the early 1840s, he was asked to add a bass aria to *Norma* (and convincing pseudo-Bellini it is too), and his first operatic success, *Rienzi*, was described by Hans von Bülow as Meyerbeer's finest work! Instead, Wagner deliberately chose another, far more difficult path, and spent his life following it.

In the three operas that followed *Rienzi* - *Der fliegende Holländer*, *Tannhäuser* and *Lohengrin* - Wagner moved further and further into uncharted territory. After writing *Lohengrin*, which was performed in 1850, there was a pause of singular importance. For five years he wrote practically no music: then he composed *Das Rheingold*. Western music would never be the same again. After *Rheingold* came *Die Walküre*, two-thirds of *Siegfried* and *Tristan und Isolde*, but none of these ground-breaking works was seen or heard on the stage until *Tristan* was performed in 1865, followed by *Die Meistersinger von Nürnberg* in 1868. Only in 1869 did *Rheingold* receive its first performance, fifteen years after its composition, and then at the insistence of King Ludwig II and against the wishes of the composer. Wagner wanted to wait until *The Ring* could be performed in its entirety. *Die Walküre* followed to the stage in 1870, again at Ludwig's insistence and despite Wagner's opposition. *Siegfried* and *Götterdämmerung* were not performed until 1876, on the completion of the Bayreuth theatre. That any artist could remain true to his goals and to himself over such a long time and in such testing circumstances is, in itself, a cause for admiration.

PREFACE

If ever there was a work of art uniquely suited to the end of one millennium and start of another, it is *Der Ring des Nibelungen*. During the course of its four dramas it describes how greed and the lust for power lead inevitably to destruction. However, it also points the way to a new beginning based on hope and love.

This book has been written to coincide with the production of *The Ring* by The State Opera of South Australia, in Adelaide in November and December 1998. For those who are unfamiliar with Wagner's greatest work, I hope that it will encourage further reading. I hope too that readers who are already acquainted with it will find what I have to say at least thought-provoking.

My own enthusiasm for *The Ring* is unabated after more than thirty years of discovery. I can still recall my delight on first hearing this remarkable music, and I am glad to say that, even after repeated hearings, it is still possible to re-awaken some of those original feelings, and to go on finding new beauties in the score and new perspectives on the drama.

Stephen Phillips, the General Director of The State Opera of South Australia and Managing Director of The State Opera Ring Corporation, suggested that I undertake pre-performance lectures from which this book has sprung, and he has generously written the Foreword; Bill Gillespie, Artistic Director of the Adelaide *Ring*, read the manuscript in draft and offered valuable comments; and Mary Rose Collom also proofread it and made useful suggestions. Christine Rothauser has kindly allowed me to use illustrations from her collection. I am most grateful to them all.

Peter Bassett
Adelaide
July 1998

Wotan rides through storm clouds, accompanied by his ravens. Lithograph by Hugo Braune, 1910–1911

An Introduction to
Der Ring des Nibelungen

When Wagner wrote the last note of the orchestral score of *Der Ring des Nibelungen* in November 1874, he completed a creative process that had begun twenty-six years earlier. The scale and scope of *The Ring* was certainly unprecedented, and it is often said (mainly, I think, to frighten new-comers to the work) that a continuous performance of all four dramas would last around fifteen hours. However, if length were *The Ring's* only claim to fame, it might not have survived beyond the nineteenth century.

So, why does *The Ring* continue to exercise such a powerful fascination a century-and-a-quarter after its first performance? Firstly, because of its music. Most people know the popular excerpts which get regular airing in the concert hall, on recordings and in films – the Ride of the Valkyries, Siegmund's Spring Song, Siegfried's Funeral Music and so on. But the music of *The Ring* is exceptional for reasons other than big tunes or exotic instrumentation. It is unusually expressive and conveys ideas and emotions in what might be called a stream of consciousness. One critic from *The Times* who attended the first complete performance in 1876 likened the music to 'a wind that is always blowing, or a stream that is always flowing'; a rather nice analogy. Generally, the music follows the words, amplifying and illustrating them, but in many instances it functions quite independently of the words, commenting on them and drawing attention to unspoken ideas and implications. It even contradicts them when this is required by the drama, say, to express differences between what is being thought and what is being said. So, it is not sufficient to rely on the libretto or surtitles in order to know what is going on.

The orchestra in *The Ring* pours out information unceasingly, even when the action is static and the singers are completely mute. This phenomenon reaches its ultimate sophistication in *Götterdämmerung* where, in Ernest Newman's words, 'the course of the drama is told with absolute clearness in the orchestra itself'. When, in Act Two of *Siegfried*, the adolescent hero hears the Woodbird and tries to communicate with it, he is unable to understand its meaning until he has tasted the dragon's blood. Understanding *The Ring* is all about 'tasting the dragon's blood'; that is, being able to 'tune in' to Wagner's highly expressive musical language.

The second reason for *The Ring's* drawing power is, I suspect, the fact that it is a drama of ideas. It belongs to no particular period and can be applied to a variety of social and political circumstances. It uses Germanic and Norse mythology to present, symbolically, the corruption of human society dominated by a lust for power. The mythological narrative draws on archetypes that are recognisable in most cultures, even if their outward manifestations vary. And so, *The Ring* is about us all.

As a young man, Wagner had been very critical of what he regarded as the degeneration of opera during the early nineteenth century into mere entertainment and triviality. 'When today we talk of opera music, in any strict sense,' he said, 'we no longer speak of an art, but of a mere article of fashion.' He was scathing about contemporary audiences who were only interested in amusement. 'Part of this amusement,' he said,

> was formed by the music sung upon the stage, to which one listened from time to time in pauses of the conversation. During the conversation and visits paid from box to box the music still went on, and with the same purpose as one assigns to table music at grand dinners, namely, to encourage by its noise the otherwise timid talk.[1]

Not surprisingly then, it is to Wagner that we owe the practice of darkening the theatre during a performance and directing everyone's eyes to the stage. The Wagnerian audience is expected to pay attention.

His aim in 1853 when composing *Das Rheingold* was to make the music serve the purpose of the drama; that is to say, not just to decorate some flimsy story line but to respond to the essence of what was being said or done on the stage. By the time he reached *Götterdämmerung*, twenty years later, the music of that tremendous work had itself become the principal vehicle for the drama.

Franz Liszt, who was two years older than Wagner, was one of his most perceptive champions. They first met in Paris in 1840, when Liszt was already a great virtuoso, sought after by elegant society and extremely wealthy. The twenty-seven-year-old Wagner on the other hand was struggling to keep himself from starvation by doing musical hackwork. After an initial flirtation with the popular genre of contemporary grand opera he decided, with characteristic egocentricity, that if the world did not appreciate what he was trying to do, then it was the world that would have to change. Liszt admired both his conviction and his music and, in 1850, took charge of the first production of *Lohengrin* in Weimar, when Wagner was in exile in Switzerland. 'Right from his first operas, but especially in *Lohengrin*,' said Liszt,

> Wagner has always mixed a different palette for each of his main characters. The more attentively you study this latest score, the more you realise what an interdependence he has created between his text and his orchestra. Not only has he personified in his melodies the feelings and passions which he has set in train ... it was also his wish that their basic features should be underlined by a corresponding orchestral colouring, and as he creates rhythms and melodies to fit the character of the people he portrays, so also he chooses the right kinds of sound to go with them.[2]

Lohengrin was a very progressive work for its time, but it had not entirely thrown off established operatic conventions. That step came with *Das Rheingold*, which was a watershed in Wagner's compositional output and in the history of music in general. In short, it was revolutionary. Any opera-lover coming to it for the first time can sense this, and getting to know it is an exciting experience.

To demonstrate how Wagner developed further the techniques which Liszt so admired, let us look at the way in which he dealt with three different groups of lesser characters in *The Ring*. They are all female, so their voices are similar, but the musical handling of each group is utterly distinctive, as their different natures demand.

Firstly, consider the three Rhinedaughters, naive watery beings usually called Rhinemaidens in English. Let us imagine ourselves in the theatre's darkness. Out of the silence comes the wondrous prelude to *Das Rheingold* evoking the depths of the River Rhine in 136 bars of increasingly fluid figurations of the chord of E flat major. The first voice that we hear is that of the Rhinemaiden Woglinde, but the melody that she sings does not continue the E flat tonality to which our ear has grown accustomed, but moves to that of A flat. The effect created by this abrupt harmonic change and the sudden withdrawal of the surging orchestral sound is that Woglinde is weightless and floating; which indeed she is supposed to be.

The Rhinemaidens' liquid and beguiling music contrasts with that of the nine Valkyries, who appear *en masse* in the third Act of *Die Walküre*. Their music is loud and violent and rather hysterical, epithets which fit precisely the Valkyries of Norse legend who were demons of death attended by storms. They scoured the battlefields gathering up dead heroes. Wagner gave them his own names, but in mythology they bore names such as 'Shrieking', 'Screaming' and 'Raging'. Listening to this music we know exactly why. It is, incidentally, a good example of Wagner the contrapuntist: at times, it combines simultaneously eight individual vocal lines.

Different again from the Rhinemaidens and the Valkyries are the three Norns, who appear in the prologue to *Götterdämmerung*. They are like the fates of Greek legend, old and wise, spinning the thread of world knowledge which binds past, present and future. They belong to all time and no time and their music does too.

Nothing even remotely like *The Ring* had existed previously in the European operatic tradition, and yet, paradoxically, it drew from some of the deepest well-springs of European culture. One of these is ancient Greek tragedy. Even as a schoolboy learning Greek, Wagner had been fascinated by the ancient world and, in later years, he studied the works of Aeschylus, Sophocles and Euripides in translation. The form of *The Ring* owes much to his view of these works, especially the *Oresteia* and *Prometheus Bound* of Aeschylus. There are some telling points in common between the classical tragedies and *The Ring*, and an awareness of them helps to explain Wagner's motivations.

The subjects of Greek tragedy were almost always taken from legend and legendary history, as was the subject of *The Ring*. The usual format offered was a tetralogy of three tragedies and a lighter 'satyric' drama. In the works of Aeschylus, the four plays dealt with different stages of the same story, just like *The Ring*. The purpose of Greek tragedy was not the frivolous one of mere entertainment and spectacle. Its emphasis was civic, that is, it dealt with issues that had vital implications for the state or society as a whole, as does *The Ring*. In classical drama, the family was often the focus for tragic action, as it certainly is in *The Ring*, and the extreme passions of love, hatred, matricide, patricide, fratricide, adultery, jealousy and even incest, to be found in the ancient plays, all resonate powerfully in *The Ring*.

Although the classical narrative was concerned with great

issues and mythological happenings, invariably the Greek dramatists also dealt with the psychological forces which shape human behaviour, and the ways in which men and women cope with events beyond their control – again prominent themes in *The Ring*.

The Greek chorus commented, reflected and made forecasts. Sometimes it was used to sound the *leitmotiv*, or recurrent theme, of the play. If, for instance, the story involved the working of an inherited trait which brought ruin on the members of a family, that motif is sounded by the chorus at appropriate points in the drama as a reminder; just as the motif of Alberich's curse, for example, is used to colour the music of *The Ring*. We can see therefore, that *The Ring* orchestra, which comments on the action, weaving 'motifs of reminiscence' as Wagner called them and providing transitional interludes, has a distant ancestor in the Greek chorus.

Wagner's detailed stage directions are often dismissed as impractical or old-fashioned, and therefore to be treated as if they were never written. This misses the point. The scenery and props of the Athenian theatre were of the simplest kind, but that did not deter Aeschylus from specifying that Prometheus be shackled to a peak in the Caucasus while conversing with the priestess Io, who had been turned into a cow! The drama was an enactment of a well-known story and the audience understood the setting even if this was only suggested by conventional scenic devices. Similarly, in much later European dramas, such as medieval miracle plays, the poet had no hesitation in setting a scene (with the most rudimentary props) in Heaven or Hell or on the deck of Noah's Ark supposedly crowded with every kind of beast. The miracle play *Noah's Flood* begins with the stage direction: '*And first in some high place, or in the clouds if it may be, God speaketh unto Noah standing without the Ark with all his family.*' Compare this with Wagner's directions for the second scene of *Das Rheingold*: '*When the mist has completely vanished aloft in gentle little clouds, in the dawning light an open space on a mountain height becomes visible. The daybreak illuminates with increasing brightness a castle with gleaming battlements ...'*

Of course, in *Das Rheingold*, Wagner seems to be asking rather a lot of the production designer, requiring the action to be first on the bed of a river, then on a mountain top, then deep in the bowels of the earth, back to the mountain top and finally on a rainbow. Some demands of the other *Ring* dramas seem equally impossible, notably in the final scene of *Götterdämmerung* where the heroine is required to ride a horse into a funeral pyre, to be followed by conflagrations in heaven and earth, collapsing buildings and an overflowing Rhine! But it seems to me that these fantastic directions are essentially no different from those of the classical and medieval dramatists or, indeed, of Shakespeare, whom Wagner idolised. Shakespeare did not think twice about locating his scenes in the midst of battle, on ships at sea and in fairy-filled forests when, in fact, Elizabethan audiences expected to see nothing more tangible than the actors in contemporary dress and a few props on a bare stage. Audiences in earlier centuries were quite used to seeing with their mind's eye and, indeed, to drawing parallels between events in the drama and events in their own time. Today we, who are less practised in these skills, partly because of the impact of cinematic literalism, call that sort of treatment 'minimalist'. I do think that, when it comes to staging *The Ring*, less is more, so that the music can work its magic in an unencumbered way.

After being greatly dissatisfied with the first complete production of *The Ring*, which he had personally supervised to the smallest detail, Wagner himself sensed that an audience might come closest to an ideal understanding of his intentions if they were willing to see with their ears, so to speak. Indeed, he joked that having invented the invisible orchestra (a reference to the sunken orchestra pit at Bayreuth) he wished he could invent the invisible theatre! It was left to Adolphe Appia and Wagner's grandson, Wieland, to demonstrate that the music uses so expressive a language that any attempt to duplicate its inner visions for the eye risks diminishing them. Most modern directors now accept this view as axiomatic.

Richard Wagner believed that music could go beyond the power of the spoken word to stir emotions, unlock sub-conscious feelings and repressed desires, appeal to widely-shared sensibilities, and convey a sense of character and even the physical environment. It was the dramatist's ultimate mode of expression.

Where did this idea come from? From a number of sources but in particular from his response as a teenager to the music of Beethoven. He was especially taken by the mysterious opening of the *Ninth Symphony*, in which Beethoven seems to be assembling the building blocks of the cosmos and bringing order out of chaos. Wagner and Beethoven were contemporaries, although they never met. Wagner was fourteen when Beethoven died. The young Richard had been drawn to music at an early age and was particularly enamoured of the works of Carl Maria von Weber, especially *Der Freischütz*. But it was his exposure to Beethoven's music that made the greatest impression on him. Later, he characterised this exposure as 'shattering'. He drew particular significance from the fact that, in the last movement of the *Ninth Symphony* the 'absolute' music had taken voice, and he saw in this an anticipation of his own objectives in the realm of music drama.

Wagner records that in Leipzig, where he lived, the *Ninth Symphony* was regarded by many as the raving of a semi-madman. Nevertheless, Wagner at the age of seventeen was so taken by it that he carefully transcribed the full score and then made a piano arrangement which he tried, unsuccessfully, to sell to the music publisher Schott. He did not actually hear a performance of the *Symphony* until the following year but it was the one work, apart from his own, with which he was most closely involved throughout his life. He conducted it many times including, symbolically, after the laying of the cornerstone of his own theatre in Bayreuth in 1872.

After finishing *Lohengrin* when he was thirty-five, Wagner did not write any music for five years. All this time he was brooding on how best to handle a subject which had long been at the back of his mind: the story of the German legendary figure, Siegfried, also known as Sigurd in Norse mythology. It was a story that was extremely popular at the time, and even Mendelssohn toyed with the idea of setting it to music. Another composer, Heinrich Dorn, actually wrote a five-act opera called *Die Nibelungen* (*The Nibelungs*), which was produced by Liszt in 1854 with Wagner's niece, Johanna, as Brünnhilde. In 1848, Wagner wrote a prose sketch setting out his ideas, then a prose scenario and then a three-act poetic drama which he called *Siegfrieds Tod* (*Siegfried's Death*). This would eventually become the basis of *Götterdämmerung* (*Twilight of the Gods*).

It was Wagner's practice to gather friends and acquaintances together and read his dramatic texts to them. This was partly to awaken interest in his work but it also gave him audience feedback at an early stage on the structure and dramatic impact of his ideas, before he moved on to the music. After one of these readings of the prose sketch of *Siegfrieds Tod*, a remark by an actor friend led him to add what is now the prologue to *Götterdämmerung*, during which the Norns recount, from their perspective, the story of events up to that point.

The repeated re-telling of the story from various perspectives is an often-criticised feature of *The Ring*. It occurs in one form or another in each of the dramas and, to a modern listener impatient for action, this can seem an unnecessary hold-up. However, the practice of repetition has a respectable lineage in oral story-telling and epic poetry, where it is used as an *aide-*

mémoire. Although the four parts of *The Ring* are aspects of a great whole, they are performed over an extended period and can be staged as entirely separate dramas. Consequently, each work needs to have some narrative overlap with the others. Repetition has another use as well. In our own time, we are familiar with the convention in detective stories which allows different individuals to describe the same events through the lens of their own recollections or self-interest. The recapitulations in *The Ring* are of interest not so much for their story content as for the light which they throw on the character of each narrator. From the composer's perspective, they also provide an opportunity to draw attention to musical themes and to reinforce these in our minds, just as the teller of an epic poem might use repeated verbal imagery to reinforce the qualities of a character or place. This is an important feature in both the *Iliad* and the *Odyssey* for example.

In May 1851, Wagner wrote to a friend:

> All through last Winter I was plagued by an idea which lately has taken possession of me to such an extent that I must bring it to fruition. Did I not once write to you with regard to a lively subject? It was that of the youth who sets out to 'learn what fear is' and is so stupid that he never manages to learn. Imagine how startled I was when I realised that this youth is no other than – the young Siegfried, who wins the Hoard and awakes Brünnhilde! The plan is now ready. I am gathering my strength together to write next month the poem of The Young Siegfried.

This work, he decided, would enable him to put visibly before his audience, and develop musically, many more details of the struggle for power than would have been possible in only one drama. What's more, *Der junge Siegfried* (*The Young Siegfried*), which we know simply as *Siegfried,* would provide an exuberant foil to the tragic atmosphere of *Siegfrieds Tod.*

Late in 1851 Wagner came to the conclusion that the wealth of mythological material explaining events leading to Siegfried's birth was so great that it could only be dealt with satisfactorily by writing yet another full-scale work and a 'big prelude', to use his own description. The new work he at first called *Siegmund and Sieglinde: The Punishment of the Valkyrie*. His dramatic sense soon told him that this title was far too long so he renamed it *The Valkyrie*. The 'big prelude' he called *The Theft of the Rhinegold* (its title reminiscent of the satyr play *Prometheus the Fire-kindler*, by Aeschylus, about the theft of fire), simplifying this in due course to *The Rhinegold*. And so it happened that the plots of the four *Ring* dramas were created more or less in reverse order. Wagner then set about composing the music in the correct order.

Synopsis

Der Ring des Nibelungen
(The Ring of the Nibelung)
A Stage Festival Play for Three Days and a Preliminary Evening

Das Rheingold (*The Rhinegold*) – The Preliminary Evening

Deep in the River Rhine, three Rhinemaidens watch over their gold. Alberich (the Nibelung of the title) lusts after them. He learns that whoever renounces love and fashions a powerful ring from the gold can rule the world. In frustration, he renounces love and snatches the gold.

High on a mountain top, the god Wotan and his wife Fricka contemplate a gleaming fortress – Valhalla, an abode for gods and heroes, built by the giants Fasolt and Fafner. The giants had been promised the goddess Freia, keeper of the golden apples of eternal youth, as payment. But Wotan is reluctant to part with Freia since, without her apples, the gods will wither and grow old. Loge, demigod of fire and an accomplished trickster, provides a solution when he tells of Alberich's theft of the gold and manufacture of the ring.

Wotan and Loge climb down through a rocky cleft to Nibelheim, where Alberich's brother Mime and the other Nibelungs are enslaved, mining gold and working metals. Through Loge's trickery, Wotan takes Alberich prisoner and they all return to the surface. Wotan seizes the ring.

A bitter Alberich curses the ring and all who possess it. Instead of Freia, the giants agree to accept the Nibelung treasure, the ring and the Tarnhelm – a magic helmet which enables the wearer to change shape at will. Reluctantly, Wotan is persuaded to give up the ring by Erda, who warns him that the end of the gods is at hand. Almost at once, the giants quarrel over their prize and Fafner kills his brother. So Alberich's curse claims its first victim. The god Donner calls up the mists and Froh conjures up a rainbow bridge to Valhalla. As Wotan devises a plan to recover the ring and Loge looks on disdainfully, the gods pass into Valhalla triumphantly, insensitive to the lament of the Rhinemaidens below.

Die Walküre (*The Valkyrie*) – The First Day

Act I

A man is being pursued through the forest during a stormy night and takes refuge, unwittingly, in the house of an enemy. Hunding, the owner, is absent but his wife takes pity on the stranger, and a bond starts to grow between them. Hunding returns and guesses the identity of his guest who recounts the story of his childhood, the murder of his mother, the abduction of his twin sister and separation from his father, Wolf. The laws of hospitality protect the guest for the night but Hunding challenges him to combat the following day, and then retires with a drink in which his wife has put a sleeping draught. The stranger recalls his father's promise to provide him with a sword in his direst need. The woman draws attention to a sword buried in the trunk of an ash tree which grows through the centre of the house. She says that the sword had been put there by a one-eyed stranger during her wedding to Hunding, and no-one had been able to draw it out.

Passionate feelings grow between the guest and the woman and eventually she realises that he is the Volsung for whom the sword was intended. She names him Siegmund. He pulls the sword from the tree with a mighty wrench and calls it *Notung* – Needful. She tells him that she is his twin sister Sieglinde and they embrace ecstatically.

Act II
While Siegmund and Sieglinde flee from Hunding, Wotan instructs his favourite Valkyrie daughter, Brünnhilde, to give victory to Siegmund in the impending fight against Hunding. Fricka, who is the guardian of marriage, is outraged, denounces the incestuous couple and castigates the promiscuous Wotan for not upholding divine law. Reluctantly, he agrees to give victory to Hunding. Wotan reveals to Brünnhilde his despair in the face of a declining, imprisoning destiny. He explains to her why they are bound to act against his own son, and demands her obedience.

Brünnhilde appears to Siegmund and tells him to prepare for death and a place in Valhalla – without Sieglinde. Moved by Siegmund's defiant response, Brünnhilde in turn decides to defy Wotan and to let Siegmund win. However, Wotan intervenes in the battle, Siegmund's sword is broken on Wotan's spear and Hunding plunges his spear into the unarmed man's chest. Bitterly, Wotan strikes Hunding dead with a wave of his hand. Brünnhilde flees Wotan's wrath, taking with her the pregnant Sieglinde and the broken pieces of the sword.

Act III
On a wild mountain summit, Brünnhilde seeks refuge with her eight Valkyrie sisters. She tells Sieglinde to flee into the forest, gives her the pieces of the sword and informs her that she will bear the noblest hero, who will be named Siegfried. Wotan catches up with Brünnhilde and condemns her to mortality, to be left asleep and vulnerable to the first man who finds her. However, he is moved by her plea that she knew that he loved Siegmund and was only doing what he himself wanted in his heart. With great emotion, he bids her farewell and encircles her with magic fire through which only one who knows no fear will be able to pass.

Siegfried – The Second Day

Act I
Sieglinde has died giving birth to Siegfried. The boy has been raised in a remote part of the forest by the Nibelung Mime. Beyond Mine's forge in the forest, Fafner, in the guise of a dragon, guards his hoard and the ring. Siegfried has observed that all of the creatures of the forest resemble their parents and scoffs at the idea that Mime could be his father. Eventually, he is told the truth about his birth. Mime despairs of repairing the shattered sword *Notung*, with which he hopes Siegfried will recover the ring. Mime learns from the Wanderer (Wotan) that the sword can be restored only by one who does not know fear. Siegfried reforges *Notung*.

Act II
Mime leads Siegfried to Fafner's cave. Resting under the green canopy of the forest, Siegfried wonders what his parents were like and if all human mothers die giving birth. He longs for congenial company and tries to communicate even with the birds of the forest. He awakens Fafner and, in the ensuing fight, kills him. Mime and Alberich squabble over who should get the treasure. When Siegfried involuntarily tastes Fafner's blood, he is able to understand the Woodbird's song and also Mime's murderous intentions. He kills Mime and then sets off towards the place where, the bird tells him, he will find a companion – Brünnhilde – who lies asleep.

Act III
The Wanderer summons Erda, demanding of her whether his destiny can be changed. She is evasive and he accepts that the future now belongs to Siegfried. The young man arrives and the Wanderer stands in his way, seeing for himself that Siegfried is

without fear and unaided. Wotan's spear yields to the sword it had shattered. After passing through the circle of fire, Siegfried awakens Brünnhilde with a kiss. At his first sight of a woman, he is alarmed and confused, but love stirs within them both. Siegfried and the now mortal Brünnhilde declare their love in terms of the utmost rapture.

Götterdämmerung (*Twilight of the Gods*) – The Third Day

Prologue and Act I
The three Norns have spun the rope of world knowledge which binds past, present and future. They tell each other why they can no longer spin. The rope breaks in a premonition of the end of the existing order. Siegfried gives Brünnhilde the ring as a token of his love and sets off towards the Rhine, in search of adventure.

At a hall on the banks of the Rhine live the Gibichung rulers, Gunther and Gutrune, and their half-brother Hagen, the son of Alberich. Hagen urges Gunther and Gutrune to find partners and proposes Siegfried for Gutrune and Brünnhilde for Gunther. Siegfried arrives and is given a potion which blocks out the memory of Brünnhilde. Meanwhile, Brünnhilde rejects the pleas of her sister, the Valkyrie Waltraute, to free the gods from their impending doom by returning the cursed ring to the Rhinemaidens. To Brünnhilde, the ring symbolises Siegfried's love for her. Siegfried disguises himself as Gunther by means of the Tarnhelm, penetrates the ring of fire, seizes the ring and abducts Brünnhilde to be Gunther's bride.

Act II
Hagen, slumbering on watch as he awaits the return of Siegfried and Gunther, is visited by his father Alberich who urges him to win back the ring for him. When, at the Gibichung court,

Brünnhilde sees the ring in Siegfried's possession, she concludes that he has betrayed her. Misunderstanding her accusation, he swears on the point of Hagen's spear that he has not betrayed Gunther's trust and offers his body to the spear if he is lying. In turn, Brünnhilde, roused to fury, dedicates the blade to his downfall. Hagen plots Siegfried's death which will be made to look like a hunting accident. Brünnhilde and Gunther demand vengeance and Hagen invokes the spirit of his father Alberich, whose curse is about to claim another victim.

Act III
During the hunt, Siegfried strays from the rest of the party to the river, where the Rhinemaidens try to persuade him to return the ring. He rebuffs them and rejoins the hunting party. He recounts the story of Mime, Notung, Fafner and the Woodbird. Hagen drops an antidote into Siegfried's drink and, gradually, as he speaks, his memory returns. When he recalls how he passed through the fire to Brünnhilde and embraced her, it is Gunther who now feels betrayed. Hagen plunges his spear into Siegfried's back. Siegfried dies with the name of his beloved Brünnhilde on his lips, and is carried back to the hall of the Gibichungs.

Hagen kills Gunther in a fight over the ring. Brünnhilde interrupts the mourning. She understands Wotan's wish to end the rule of the gods and extinguish the curse which has now claimed her innocent lover. She directs the building of a funeral pyre and, taking the ring, joins Siegfried in the flames. The Rhine overflows its banks and, in the heavens, Valhalla itself is seen consumed by fire. The Rinemaidens swim on the flood to reclaim the ring and, as Hagen tries to seize it, they drag him down into the depths. Thus the old order passes away. In its place is a cleansed world and the promise of a new beginning.

Wotan is the key figure around whom the whole of the drama of The Ring *unfolds. Wagner based his Wotan on the Norse god Odin, shown here with his one eye and his ravens, Huginn, who represented Thought, and Muninn, who represented Memory. The ravens kept Odin/Wotan informed of what was happening in the world. Illustration from* The Prose Edda, *1760*

Das Rheingold

The beginning of *Das Rheingold*, like that of Beethoven's *Ninth Symphony*, suggests a darkness over the face of the deep; a primal state of creation. But whereas Beethoven seems to be assembling his universe from discrete musical molecules, Wagner's creation grows organically out of a single cell, a sustained deep E flat on the double-basses. After what seems a long time, this cell begins to divide into the components of that most basic entity in music, the major chord. Spread out melodically as an arpeggio by the horns, this forms what might be called the basic motif of Nature. As it continues to grow, a gently undulating theme appears in the strings, and then the whole motif begins to travel at twice the speed, acquiring the unmistakable motion of flowing water – the River Rhine, in whose depths the whole drama begins.

The prelude to *Das Rheingold* lasts about four-and-a-quarter minutes, and the listener is gradually overtaken by a sense of timelessness. Only the startling sound of the Rhinemaiden's voice breaks the spell and brings us abruptly into a more recognisable world. The transition, as Warren Darcy has noted,[1] is from timelessness to measured time, from indistinct musical shapes to distinct shapes, from simple forms of nature to human consciousness.

In one sense therefore, *The Ring* might be seen as a parable about the tragic consequences of humanity losing touch with its natural origins; a topical subject for the late twentieth century.

The most important feature of *The Ring* from a musical point of view is Wagner's use of so-called *leitmotivs*, a word usually translated as 'leading motifs'. This was not Wagner's term: he used other descriptions, including 'chief motifs', 'ground themes', 'motifs of reminiscence' and even 'melodic moments of feeling'. Whatever name we give them, they are themes associated with characters, objects, events and emotions. They are usually quite short and, in essence, melodic, and they are capable of the most subtle manipulation. They can be used in their basic form, which is how we first encounter them, or they can be modified or hybridised through a kind of musical genetic engineering, to reflect particular developments in the drama. They can be superimposed one upon another or turned upside down to imply their opposite. Sometimes it is sufficient to hint at them by using just their rhythms, their general shape, or an associated harmony or instrumental colour. In the continuous flow of the music (the so-called endless melody, unbroken by conventional arias, recitative, ensembles and the like) even the most fleeting reference can be sufficient to reveal some point or consideration relevant to the story. As well as reminding us of things past, the *leitmotivs* can also be used to foreshadow things to come, preparing our emotions for some action or visual image.

Consider one or two straightforward examples of the way in which Wagner manipulates his musical themes. Water and earth are both manifestations of nature and so one would expect to find some thematic connection between them. Sure enough, the motif of Erda, the all-wise earth spirit, is clearly derived from the nature motif, but in the process it has moved from a major to a minor mode and from flowing 6/8 time to the solid 4/4 of *terra firma*. In *Das Rheingold*, Erda is roused from eternal slumbers to warn Wotan and the other gods that the ring will seal their fate and that everything they represent has been compromised and is coming to an end. The antithesis of creation is destruction, so the nature motif, which has already been transformed in connection with Erda, is turned upside down as she warns of the end of the gods.

The motifs of the gold and the ring are, obviously, of central importance. The gold motif is derived from the nature motif, as is the motif of the ring. But whereas the motifs of nature and the gold use benign major chords, the notes of the ring motif make up a chromatic dissonance in the minor key. The life-giving gold has become a death-dealing ring.

To discover how Wagner's motifs mutate in the context of the drama, it is useful to look at what happens to, say, the ring motif in different circumstances. At the beginning of *Siegfried* for example, we are made aware musically of Mime's scheming, even before the curtain rises, and we can tell just from the harmonies, which are those of the ring motif, what this scheming is all about. Through the music we read Mime's mind. By the time we get to *Götterdämmerung*, the motif has evolved further in relation to Hagen. The dissonance that we hear at the beginning of this transformed motif permeates *Götterdämmerung*, suggesting a state of progressive decline.

One could go on in a similar vein pointing out connections and derivations of this kind in relation to a whole host of motifs. In some cases, one motif acts upon another, producing an independent musical offspring. In a letter of 1854, Wagner observed that *Das Rheingold* had become a close-knit unity. 'There is scarcely a bar in the orchestra,' he said, 'that does not develop out of preceding motifs'.[2] Other thematic families have been identified and given labels, such as those of Wotan's spear, love, heroic humanity, the sword, the inspiring power of women, magic and mystery, and so on. The total number of motifs has varied in different calculations from 82 to as many as 367. It is interesting to play 'spot the connection' and people have been doing this ever since Hans von Wolzogen produced a guide book on the subject in the late nineteenth century. Ultimately though, the names of the motifs are just convenient labels. They were not used by Wagner and they do him a disservice if they lead people to think that the *leitmotiv* is only a musical signpost, introduced at appropriate times to assist with comprehension of the drama.

Undoubtedly, the musical ideas – those 'melodic moments of feeling' – which Wagner devised were intended to have a dramatic and narrative function. However, they were far from arbitrary and he did not set them out in advance like pieces of coloured fabric ready to be assembled into a patchwork quilt. Indeed, many of his ideas seem to have evolved during the process of composition.

During the course of a performance, it is hardly practicable to try to pick out and name various motifs as they appear, evolve and disappear in the musical stream, any more than one would consciously name the changing moods of a companion or the passing features of a landscape. We register such things intuitively and absorb them unconsciously. However, familiarity makes us more aware of them, and so it is with the music of *The Ring*.

Wagner's particular skill as a composer was two-fold. Firstly, he exploited his rich thematic material with consummate mastery. He was proud, and rightly so, of the subtlety with which his themes were interwoven and developed 'symphonically' in order to give expression to dramatic action. Secondly, he was able to create themes which not only seemed appropriate to their subject but had a powerful effect on the listener's own sense of recollection. His 'melodic moments of feeling' make an impression, not because we hear them once and so recognise them again, but because they seem familiar even when we hear them for the first time. The most obvious examples are the melodic representations of nature – the Rhine, the woodbird, the forest and so on – which strike us immediately as utterly recognisable. However, we can also identify instinctively with the musical representations of a whole range of emotions and moods.

This amalgam of the musical and the extra-musical is a potent and essential part of the Wagnerian magic, although it was anathema to Igor Stravinsky and his followers as they struggled to escape the long shadow cast by Wagner over late nineteenth- and early twentieth-century music. However, its legacy is still with us today in many forms, both popular and serious.

In *The Ring*, one particularly long shadow is cast by Alberich, the Nibelung of the title, whom we first encounter in *Das Rheingold* clambering out of an underwater cleft to watch the three Rinemaidens disporting themselves in the pristine waters of the Rhine. (This is mythology remember!) Alberich is not exactly what you would call a good catch. With his fellow Nibelungs he inhabits Nibelheim, a place of gloomy caverns and fissures beneath the earth's surface, and he smelts and smiths hard metals. Alberich is everything the Rhinemaidens are not. They are beautiful and agile; he is ugly and awkward. They are naive and playful; he is calculating and lustful. All of this is apparent from the music, as well as from the text.

Wagner's texts combine archaic and modern language and even words of his own invention, because he saw words and music as two sides of the one dramatic coin. One feeds from the other. In *The Ring*, unlike his earlier works, the lines are short and declamatory and use alliteration rather than end rhyme. All of these features are immediately apparent from the very first words that we hear in *Rheingold*: *Weia! Waga! Woge, du Welle!* The use of alliteration, known as *Stabreim*, is frequently found in old German poetry, and in old English and Latin poetry too. It allows for flexible musical treatment and it contributes to an impression of a mythological time frame.

The *Ring* exercises inexhaustible fascination as a drama of ideas, largely because of its diverse sources and influences. Greek tragedy, Germanic and Norse mythology, the writings of nineteenth-century philosophers such as Feuerbach and Schopenhauer, the 1849 Dresden uprising and its brutal suppression, were all fuel for the restless and inventive mind of Richard Wagner. Consequently, it has been possible to interpret *The Ring* from just about any political or sociological perspective, a fact which stage directors have found particularly useful.

Alberich personifies an all-too-human craving for wealth and influence at any cost. You will notice how easily he renounces love when the Rhinemaidens let slip that by doing so he can have world dominion. The important motif of the renunciation of love reappears many times in different forms throughout *The Ring*, with telling effect.

Some might say that Alberich is just getting his priorities right, subscribing to the modern notion that power is the ultimate aphrodisiac. He manages to beget an ungodly son, Hagen, by buying a human partner, and that will ultimately lead back to the Rhine, to the murder of Siegfried and the return of the ring to the Rhinemaidens. So things come full circle, but at a price. It is worth listening closely to the way in which Wagner describes the rape of the gold, the frenzied despair of the Rhinemaidens and the atmosphere of foreboding which descends on an unsuspecting world.

Das Rheingold was written to be performed without intervals or even the closing of the curtain. To effect his scene-changes, Wagner wrote transitional passages which were masterpieces of musical description. From the depths of the Rhine, plunged into darkness by the theft of the gold, he takes us up into less watery realms, up, with occasional echoes of grief through mists and fogs, to the bright sun-lit atmosphere of a very high place where the chief god Wotan and his consort Fricka are slumbering on a flowery bank. The towers of Valhalla, built by the giants Fasolt and Fafner at Wotan's behest, gleam in the rays of the rising sun, and the hymnlike Valhalla motif, implying the majesty of the gods, resounds in the brass. This motif will be used from here on to refer to the gods and, in particular, to Wotan.

But all is not sweetness and light. The liquid, plaintive music of the Rhinemaidens and the slippery, pungent music of Alberich have given way to a brittle mood of marital stress and strain. Wotan and Fricka are definitely in need of some marriage guidance counselling. We cannot really blame Fricka of course. Her husband is a notorious philanderer, like Zeus in Greek mythology and, as payment for building Valhalla, he has even promised to hand over her sister Freia, the goddess of youth and love, to the brutish giants. In Norse mythology, the giants were implacable enemies of the gods. In a sense then, Wotan too has renounced love by offering Freia as the price for Valhalla. Fricka goes on and on about foolish schemes and about men making decisions without consulting the women. For his part, Wotan's preoccupation is with grand plans and ambitions and the challenge of ruling the world. Wagner's own experiences with his first wife Minna must have seemed all too relevant when he was writing Scene Two of *Das Rheingold*. In a letter written during the composition of *Das Rheingold*, Wagner observed:

> Alberich and his ring could not have harmed the gods unless the latter had already been susceptible to evil. Where, then, is the germ of this evil to be found? Look at the scene between Wotan and Fricka ... The firm bond which binds them both ... constrains them both to the mutual torment of a loveless union. [3]

His implication is clear: lovelessness, either deliberately chosen, as in the case of Alberich, or the product of circumstance, as in the case of Wotan and Fricka, carries the seeds of destruction. The corollary is that an act of love – especially love to the point of self-sacrifice – carries the seeds of life. In Wagner's dramas, self-sacrificing love is frequently (though not exclusively) offered by a woman, in a redeeming and life-affirming role.

Apart from Wotan and Fricka, the gods in *Das Rheingold* are rather sketchily drawn, with the exception of the demigod Loge whose element is fire. He is the most interesting character in the drama because he is clever and mercurial, and he stands apart from the others. He does their bidding and solves their problems, but he is never accepted as 'one of them' – consequently, he despises them. In dramatic terms he stands between the gods and the audience, letting us hear what is going through his mind.

We learn more of Loge's shifty character as events unfold. For example, it is Loge who, in the magnificent final scene of *Das Rheingold,* declares in a voice which only we can hear: 'They are hastening to their end, those who think they are so great ... I'm tempted to change into flames and burn them all up ... I must consider. Who knows what I shall do.' But, for all his talk, he is just an opportunist. As the gods process into Valhalla, he tells the mournful Rhinemaidens to stop their wailing. 'You might have lost your gold,' he says to them, 'but the gods' new golden splendour will shine on you instead.' Everyone laughs, except the Rhinemaidens. Loge's ethics are as shifting and insubstantial as the flickering, flame-like motif that accompanies him.

There is an interesting example in Scene Two of *Rheingold* of the subtlety of Wagner's technique in using leitmotivs to refer to a character by implication, without needing a verbal reference. At one point Wotan and the giants, Fasolt and Fafner, are discussing the contract for the building of Valhalla. Wotan is reneging on the deal to give the giants the goddess Freia and tells them to ask for some other fee. Fafner accuses his brother of having been taken in by Wotan's tricks. However, we know that the 'fine print', so to speak, in the contract was not Wotan's doing but Loge's, for it is he who personifies trickery and manipulation. It was Loge who encouraged the deal on the basis that he would find a ransom for Freia. So, when Fafner speaks of Wotan's trickery we hear, in the soft flickering music of the violas, not a reference to Wotan but one to Loge, reminding us of who was the real architect of the loophole.

When Loge appears with the much-awaited news of a means of ransoming Freia, he admits that he has searched in vain for a ransom that would compensate for the power of love. But he does say that he has heard about Alberich's renunciation of love, the theft of the Rhinegold and manufacture of the ring. The ring is referred to ten times in the orchestra during Loge's account, and Wotan becomes mesmerised by the idea of getting his hands on it. The giants decide that they would settle for Alberich's gold if this could be obtained for them.

Loge enjoys one special advantage in being an outsider. He has avoided the gods' addiction to Freia's golden apples of youth. When Freia is carried off by the giants as security for the promised gold, the other gods suffer withdrawal symptoms and begin to feel their age – which, if you are a god, is not inconsiderable! Loge observes their discomfort rather smugly. The music of this passage provides another example of Wagner's skill in evoking intangible things. How many other composers would have dared to set the ageing process to music?

One of the most exciting passages in *Das Rheingold* is that known as the descent to Nibelheim. Determined to obtain the ring and the golden hoard and wriggle out of his commitment to give Freia to the giants, Wotan decides to go with Loge down through a fissure in the rock to the subterranean caverns where Alberich has enslaved the rest of his race. It is not just a geographical journey that we undertake, although that seems real enough with its downward rush and sulphurous chromaticism. There is a psychological journey too. The motifs which drive the orchestral sound are those of Alberich forswearing the love of woman, the gold and the ring, the spurning of Alberich by the Rhinemaidens (the latter theme transforming itself into the hellish and unforgettable hammering of anvils), and once again, pervading everything, the sinister harmonies of the ring.

What happens next is a black comedy with overtones of Hieronymus Bosch. We hear the tormented shrieks of the terrified Mime and the other Nibelungs as they are whipped by the all-powerful and invisible Alberich. We see (or at least imagine with the help of the music) Alberich being tricked by Loge into transforming himself firstly into a monstrous dragon and then into a tiny toad, whereupon Wotan and Loge pounce on him. (Incidentally, this latter detail is reminiscent of the Grimms' fairy-tale of *Puss in Boots* in which the ogre is goaded into turning himself into a lion and then into a mouse, enabling the cat to pounce on him and devour him.) The gods return to the surface with Alberich bound and bitter.

Wagner's orchestration is nowhere more varied and brilliant than in this scene in Nibelheim, nor his vocal line more lively and to the point. It is a striking manifestation of his theories about *Gesamtkunstwerk*, the fusion of text, music, scene and action in the service of the drama. All of the considerable dramatic detail: the contest of wits between Loge and Alberich, Alberich's plan to rule the world, Loge's taunting of Alberich, the latter's transformations and the capture of the Nibelung are ingeniously arranged, as Warren Darcy points out, as a nine-part rondo in which a recurrent musical refrain – the rondo theme – alternates with four contrasting episodes. The refrain recurs each time in the controlling key of A major, while the episodes explore different tonalities and thematic material. In such a way, Wagner controls the varied forces which are at work in this extended scene. Here, as in many other instances in *The Ring*, the apparently free form of the work belies its carefully organised structure. This structure is disguised by the large scale of the work and the narrative function of the themes.

In the midst of all this activity, there is one rather haunting motif which is worth special mention. It is associated with the Tarnhelm or magic helmet which renders Alberich invisible and allows him to change his form at will. We are left in no doubt as to the Tarnhelm's supernatural qualities by Wagner's use of pianissimo muted horns and unworldly harmonies. This simple but very effective motif will appear in various guises throughout *The Ring* whenever magic, which is to say deceit, is afoot. It is related in form to the motif of Loge, though played very much more slowly. The logic in this, of course, is that magic, deceit and trickery are all related concepts.

Back on the surface, events are about to take a disastrous turn. Not satisfied with the golden treasure which is dragged up by the enslaved Nibelungs to ransom Alberich, Wotan demands the ring as well. The motif of his spear, symbol of his will and lawful authority, blares out on the trombones before he commits the violent and unlawful act of wrenching the ring from Alberich's finger. Thus the law-maker turns law-breaker. The spear motif is another of those primal themes that seem to mirror the physical shape of the objects they represent. It is a strong descending line of notes, like a straight shaft, uncompromising in its force and sense of authority.

Then, in one of the most vitriolic passages in all music, Alberich damns his tormentors, cursing the ring and whoever possesses it. It is amazing to think that this shocking music was written nearly a century-and-a-half ago, at the time when Verdi was writing the three great works of his middle period – *Rigoletto, Il Trovatore* and *La Traviata* – and five years before Gounod wrote *Faust*. Masterly as these works are, *Das Rheingold*, by comparison, comes from quite another world.

The sinister motif of Alberich's Curse begins with the notes of the ring motif turned upside down. The implication? That the power of the ring will be negative rather than positive, destructive rather than creative.

With the return of the giants and Freia, the gods regain their youthful appearance. As ransom for Freia, the giants demand sufficient gold to obscure her from head to toe. The gold is piled up but the goddess's hair remains visible. Loge, with great reluctance, yields the Tarnhelm to obscure it. Fasolt checks for any other gaps and catches a glint from Freia's eyes. The music suddenly takes on a soulful quality, for the uncouth giant has quite fallen for Freia and bitterly regrets having to give her up. Only the blocking out of her gaze will persuade him to depart without her. Fafner points to the ring on Wotan's finger and insists that it be handed over to fill the gap. Loge interjects that he had promised to return the ring to the Rhinemaidens but Wotan tells him to think again; he took the ring for himself and won't give it to anyone. The giants conclude that, if this is Wotan's last word, they will take Freia after all.

Amidst the pleading and confusion which follows, the all-knowing earth spirit Erda appears and tells Wotan to give up the ring. Her music looks back to the world's beginning, and forward to the end of the gods in *Götterdämmerung*. Wretchedness, doom and disaster lie in the ring, she warns. After much thought and prompting by the others, Wotan heeds her advice, and so the cursed ring passes to the giants. Almost at once it claims its first victim when Fafner slays his brother Fasolt in an argument over who should keep the ring. The orchestra reminds us of Alberich's curse.

The giants are a bit of a problem for stage directors. They have variously been depicted as Neanderthal blockheads, as rude mechanicals in the Shakespearian sense, and even as astronauts. In the Sydney production of the 1980s they resembled shaggy muppets. In the centenary production at Bayreuth, Patrice Chéreau put his singers on the shoulders of strong men, all draped in oversize costumes. The giants' music is seismic and unsubtle in the extreme. Well, no one expects them to be scintillating conversationalists and ballroom dancers, and the music gives us a fairly uncompromising picture of just what they are like, mentally and physically. They go to great trouble to win the gold, the ring and the Tarnhelm, but when the surviving giant, Fafner, gets his hands on all of these things he can think of nothing more productive to do than to transform himself into a dragon and guard them. If Alberich demonstrates the destructive consequences of craving wealth and misusing power, Fafner personifies the pointlessness of hoarding wealth and squandering power. The *Ring* is an allegory of personal, social and political behaviour, and its messages would not have been lost on Wagner's contemporaries.

In 1848, the year of the first prose sketch for *The Ring*, there were popular revolts and uprisings in Paris, Vienna, Berlin, Frankfurt and Prague, and Karl Marx published his *Communist Manifesto*. It is likely that Wagner read it or at least knew of it. Revolution was in the air and Wagner wrote to a friend that he had become so depressed with his position in Dresden where, although he was Court Conductor, he could get none of his artistic reforms approved, he had become a revolutionary – 'in thought if not in deed'. He delivered a speech to a left-wing political association in which he demanded one-man-one-vote, the abolition of inherited wealth and power, and the surrender by the aristocracy of its position of privilege. He joined the revolutionary Popular Front and was an associate of the anarchist Mikhail Bakunin. In 1849 the King of Saxony dissolved the Chambers of Deputies and soldiers opened fire on protesting Dresdeners. The government appealed for Prussian troops to assist in suppressing the revolt. Wagner had leaflets printed and distributed amongst the King's soldiers asking 'Are you on our side and against foreign troops?', and he took his post in a church tower reporting on troop movements. The revolt was brutally suppressed, a warrant was issued for Wagner's arrest and he went into exile in Switzerland. The whole experience made a lasting impression on him.

Richard Wagner was an impassioned artist, not a rational political thinker, and his revolutionary leanings were motivated primarily by his artistic frustrations. His political views stemmed from a personal resentment of certain artistically influential individuals and counter-revolutionaries, including members of the aristocracy and prominent Jews (hence his notorious essay of 1850, *Jewishness in Music*). He railed against the shallow attitude of the public towards art and harboured deep resentment over his bitter experiences as a young man in Paris, during which he and his first wife had had to pawn everything of value, even their wedding rings, and then sell the pawn tickets in order to survive. On more than one occasion in Paris (and in Riga before then), Wagner came close to being sent to a debtor's prison. (There exists a letter which, if it is to believed, shows that he did in fact end up in prison.) There is no doubt that the reform of society, in a fairly general sense, was a subject close to his heart, and this is certainly reflected in *The Ring*. Indeed, in 1852 he told his friend Theodor Uhlig that composition of *The Ring* would have to wait until 'after the revolution', for only then would the world understand the revolutionary content of the work.

Wagner does not mention Karl Marx in his writings, but Marx certainly mentions him. Nearly thirty years later, Marx was to complain 'No matter where one goes, one is plagued with the question "What do you think of Wagner?" '

There have been several notable Marxist interpretations of *The Ring* and, in 1963, the Soviet Union issued a special postage stamp to commemorate the 150th anniversary of Wagner's birth. But before we conclude that Wagner was a proto-communist, as directors in the old Eastern Europe were prone to do, or a proto-Nazi as Adolf Hitler and his friends decreed, we need to remember that *The Ring* is singularly accommodating of just about any political and social gloss that one wishes to give it. There have been *Rings* of the left, the right and the centre, *Rings* of the industrial revolution, fairytale *Rings* and environmental *Rings*. There have been *Rings* set in outer space and *Rings* with laser beams, *Rings* of a post-nuclear catastrophe and *Rings* with motor cars and rubbish bins on stage and Brünnhilde with her head in a paper bag. In short, the stagings have changed according to generation and the fantasies of individual directors, but the work itself, like John Brown's body, still goes marching on.

Returning to the plot of *Das Rheingold*, each of the gods reacts in a different and revealing way to the murder of Fasolt and the loss of the ring. Loge, ever the courtier, puts a favourable complexion on the events. You are well rid of the ring, he tells Wotan. See how your enemies are now murdering each other for the gold that you let go. Fricka turns her attention to a comfortable domestic future in her new home, the gleaming Valhalla. Gone for the moment is the nagging goddess of marriage vows; instead we see Fricka the helpmate, caressing and cajoling, urging her lord to lead her through the splendid portals. However, Wotan is not to be soothed, and responds gloomily that an evil wage has paid for their home. He frets about losing the ring and is already agonising over how he might retrieve it.

Donner, the god of thunder, decides it is time to clear the air. In purely musical terms, this means a transmutation of the B flat minor tonality associated with Alberich, and other musical elements identified with the Nibelungs, into a tonal environment more favourable to the gods. With one of those dramatic touches which reveal the composer's unerring sense of theatre, Donner whips up the clouds and creates a tremendous flash of lightning and clap of thunder. We share in the sudden release of tension. The clouds disperse and, in the evening light, a rainbow bridge stretches from the feet of Donner and his brother Froh, the god of Spring, across the Rhine gorge to Valhalla. Wotan's spirits are lifted by the glorious sight, and a 'great idea' suddenly occurs to him. The music tells us so, although we shall have to wait until *Die Walküre* to find out just what this idea is.

A procession is formed and the gods move grandly off across the rainbow bridge to happiness ever after. But their reverie is interrupted by mournful cries from the river below: 'Rhinegold! Rhinegold! Shining gold! ... For your true radiance we are mourning.' Wotan and Loge throw a few sarcastic words in the direction of the Rhinemaidens and, amidst laughter, the procession resumes with all its delusions of triumph. However, the Rhinemaidens, overwhelmed with longing for their gold, have the last word, just as they had the first: 'Goodness and truth dwell but in the waters,' they sing, 'false and base all those who dwell up above!' There speaks the authentic voice of the forty-year-old Richard Wagner, Wagner the revolutionary, for whom the artistic gods of the mid-nineteenth century were equally false and base. Those gods, like their cosmic counterparts, were much too pleased with themselves to listen; but that was about to change.

Die Walküre

If Richard Wagner had written *Die Walküre* in the 1980s instead of in the 1850s he might well have called it *Aspects of Love*, for love in its various forms is central to this most popular of the *Ring* dramas. 'Only love,' he wrote,

the union of man and woman (physical and metaphysical), creates the human being. Fulfilment comes to us only through the enjoyment of love, that most eternal of all things. The world attains complete reality for me only through a loved one and through the appearance of the beloved. This may be a child or a friend but we can only love that child or friend wholly if we already have the capacity of love. That, a man learns only through a woman. [1]

When Wagner was composing the music for *Die Walküre* his first marriage was in tatters, but he was deliriously infatuated with Mathilde Wesendonck, the wife of a German business man who lived in Zurich. The Wesendoncks became generous supporters and ardent champions of his music. The beautiful Mathilde is best remembered as his muse for *Tristan und Isolde* – that 'definitive expression of yearning and unsatisfiable desire' as Barry Millington calls it – but the manuscript of Act One of *Die Walküre*, written several years earlier, already bears testimony to the composer's infatuation. The score contains various jottings in Wagner's hand referring secretly to Mathilde. These jottings are sometimes associated with particular musical phrases and take the form of cryptic sets of initials: *i.l.d.g.* meaning in German 'I love you infinitely', and *L.d.m.M?* 'do you love me Mathilde?'. Others, once deciphered, spell out: 'Were it not for you, beloved', 'You are my all!', and 'Beloved, why have you left me?'. The delirium of love had made him rather childish and he admitted as much to Mathilde, but it also provided the catalyst for some of his greatest love music. Throughout his life, Wagner seems to have needed the strong stimuli of relationships and sensory experiences in order to conjure up his imaginary world of the emotions.

There is a common emotional thread linking Act One of *Die Walküre* and *Tristan*: a powerful sense of love and longing, made even more intense by illicit relationships. Sieglinde's offer to Siegmund of a drinking horn filled with mead in *Die Walküre*, has an obvious parallel in Isolde's offer to Tristan of the cup with its potion. While the immediate result in *Die Walküre* is less convulsive than it is in *Tristan*, the similarities are plain. Both couples drink from their respective cups. Siegmund's gaze, according to the stage directions, rests on Sieglinde with growing warmth, his expression betraying strong emotion. Tristan and Isolde gaze with deepest emotion and a growing longing into one another's eyes. And Siegmund, like Tristan, is destined for sorrow.

In the First Act of *Die Walküre* we experience intensely the joy of love's presence and the pain of love's absence. The twins, Siegmund and Sieglinde, separated in childhood, rediscover each other in a forest hut, although mutual recognition comes slowly. Siegmund arrives exhausted in the midst of a storm, fleeing from his enemies. The storm is both a natural phenomenon and a metaphor for the turmoil in his mind and soul. This startling operatic prelude would be considered audacious if penned by a composer in the late twentieth century – Wagner conceived it in 1854. The hut in which Siegmund has sought refuge is built around the trunk of an ash tree and belongs to the grim and forbidding Hunding. We can tell exactly what type of man he is from the music associated with him.

We have already seen in connection with *Das Rheingold* that marriage and happiness were far from synonymous for Wagner. In the case of Wotan and Fricka, marriage is, as envisioned by Wagner, a bond that constrains them to the mutual torment of a loveless union. How much more then is this true for Sieglinde, who has been forced to marry Hunding against her will. She offers a drink of water to the exhausted man, and a solitary cello mirrors the gentleness of her action with music of extraordinary beauty.

Then Hunding enters. His suspicions of the stranger are confirmed when Siegmund recounts the story of his flight and the sufferings of his family. When he was a boy, Siegmund says, he and his father, Wolf, returned one day from hunting to find their home burned to the ground. He refers to his home as the 'wolf's lair'. This and other wolfish references derive from the ancient myths from which Wagner drew much of his raw material. Siegmund had found his mother dead and his twin sister abducted and, eventually, he was separated from his father. A wolf's skin lay in the woods but his father was nowhere to be found. The Valhalla motif is heard in the orchestra, and we realise, even if the young man does not, that his father is the god Wotan. Siegmund continues with his narrative. He wandered as an outcast, attracting ill luck wherever he went. What he thought right others thought wrong. What he held base others considered fair. He longed for loved ones but found only enemies. Finally he was involved in a skirmish during which he killed other men. Pursued and alone, he had taken the name *Wehwalt* – Lord of Woe.

Hearing this, Hunding knows beyond doubt that they are mortal enemies, for the men killed by Siegmund were his kinsmen. Custom requires that the stranger be given sanctuary for the night, but on the morrow, Hunding insists, it will be necessary for them to settle their differences in combat.

Wagner's use of the orchestra throughout this scene is full of subtlety and revelations. The thematic structure which he had established so effectively in *Das Rheingold* now shows its great flexibility, and he is able to manipulate it with growing confidence. For example, the relationship between Hunding and those killed in battle is foreshadowed simply by use of the rhythm of Hunding's motif while Siegmund is telling his story. Again, when Hunding notices a physical resemblance between Siegmund and Sieglinde, his remarks are accompanied by an orchestral reference to the spear motif, symbol of Wotan's authority and will. Why? Because Wotan was their father and the twins, unwittingly, are the instruments of his will.

Siegmund's arrival on that stormy night had stirred deep feelings within Sieglinde (although she does not know why) and her initial reaction of sympathy grows into something stronger. Wagner gives Siegmund a theme derived from the spear motif, implying that he is far from being a free agent. As the feelings of the twins towards each other begin to grow, this is reflected by an intertwining of musical themes associated with them.

Hunding retires and Sieglinde gives him a drink laced with a sleeping draught. Siegmund, left alone by the fire, recalls his father's promise to provide a sword for him in his hour of need. In his desperation he now calls out to his father for help. From the orchestra we hear the sword motif, first heard when it blazed forth at the end of *Rheingold* when Wotan had had his 'great idea'.

While Siegmund is preoccupied with his thoughts, firelight glints on a sword buried to its hilt in the trunk of the ash tree. *We can guess its significance*: Wotan's 'great idea' had been to use his mortal offspring to regain Alberich's ring. Siegmund, armed with the sword, would do what the god, enmeshed in his treaties and laws, could not.

When Sieglinde returns, she explains how the sword was left

in the tree by a stranger who appeared at her wedding feast. No-one could draw it out, although many had tried. We can tell from the orchestra that the stranger was Wotan, and from Sieglinde's account that the sword was intended for a hero. Brother and sister grow more ardent in their exchanges and begin to use the ecstatic, compressed language which later would be taken to such extremes in *Tristan und Isolde*. Suddenly a gust of wind blows open the great door of the hut and moonlight floods into the room. 'Ah, who went there?' she cries. 'No one went, but one has come,' he answers. Siegmund describes the passing of the winter storms and the arrival of spring in music of great lyrical beauty, and Sieglinde tells her brother that *he* is the spring. In Wagner's music, love and lyricism are inseparable.

For the first time, in the moonlight, brother and sister are able to see each other clearly: they comment on their likenesses – the way they look, the way they sound – and they probe relentlessly at each other's identity. When the young man calls his father by another name, Wälse, and acknowledges his race as the Volsungs, Sieglinde tells him joyously that the sword is intended for him. She names him *Siegmund*, which means 'guardian of victory', and with a mighty effort, he pulls the sword from the tree, calling it *Notung* – 'Needful'. She reveals herself as his sister Sieglinde. Passionately he draws her to him and with music of the greatest excitement, they embrace as the curtain falls. The First Act of *Die Walküre* has few equals in its emotional appeal and dramatic construction.

There is a striking contrast between Act One of *Die Walküre* and the cosmic 'morality play' of *Das Rheingold*, where we were confronted not so much with characters as with characterisations. Instead of Wotan, Loge, Fafner and Woglinde, these *dramatis personae* of the *Ring's* Preliminary Evening might equally have been named 'Power', 'Trickery', 'Brute Force' and 'Naivety', just as in medieval morality plays one would find characters called

'Good Deeds', 'Knowledge', 'Strength' and 'Beauty'. In *Rheingold*, Love is spoken about and even renounced, but is never apparent on stage. Now in *Die Walküre*, human beings, real characters, make their appearance for the first time, and so too does human love. Even the immortals, Wotan and Fricka, who reappear on this First Day of Wagner's Festival Play (to use his terminology), are more rounded and complex characters than they had been in *Rheingold*. Of course, events have moved on. Forces have been unleashed from which neither gods nor humans can remain aloof.

In the whole scheme of the *Ring*, it might seem strange that the little domestic drama which is played out in Hunding's hut warrants a whole Act to itself. But this very fact is an indication that we are now truly in the world of men and women (albeit of divine origin), and such is the expressive power of the music that any reservations are quickly dispelled.

If a composer in our own time wrote an opera in which one of the most sympathetically handled characters drugged her husband so that she could commit adultery and incest with her brother, this would attract more than passing interest from those concerned with public morals and the corruption of minors. But that is precisely the subject of *Die Walküre*, written nearly a century-and-a-half ago and performed countless times ever since. Indeed, this work has unquestionably become the most popular of the *Ring* dramas and is often performed independently of the others. It wasn't always so. Critics at the first complete performance at Bayreuth in 1876 liked *Siegfried* best, and the Viennese critic Eduard Hanslick thought that the whole of *Walküre* should be dropped. Nevertheless, before long Wagner was complaining that this work was being promoted more than the others by touring companies.

Wilhelm Mohr, another critic present in 1876, described the brother-sister relationship as 'overpoweringly repulsive to the healthy sensibility', and *The Times* critic of the day reported that the 'matter was so objectionable to modern thought' that the very survival of the *Ring* was unlikely. He also took exception to Siegfried's marriage to the eldest of his aunts – long before Anna Russell did!

Incest: what can one say about this controversial aspect of the work? The first thing, I suppose, is that we are not talking about incest in the ordinary sense, despite the very human qualities exhibited by the sibling lovers. We are talking about mythological incest involving the children of a god, and that is a very different kettle of fish. Consider some parallels in a variety of religious traditions. The Book of Genesis provides an account of the creation of the first humans, Adam and Eve, and goes on to identify their children and grandchildren. Taking the story at face value, one can only assume that the grandchildren were the fruit of intermarriage by Adam and Eve's children. In Egyptian mythology, Osiris and Isis, brother and sister, became the parents of Horus. In Mesopotamian mythology the god Shamash was the husband and brother of Ishtar, goddess of love and fertility. Niörd, the Scandinavian spirit of water and air married his sister Nerthus. In Greek mythology, Kronos married his sister Rhea and fathered Zeus, who in turn married his own sister Hera. Elsewhere in Norse mythology, the fertility god Frey, whom Wagner calls Froh, had an incestuous relationship with his sister Freya (Freia), also a fertility figure. Unlike the taboo against literal incest which has applied in most cultures from time immemorial, incest amongst mythical beings, often to explain natural phenomena, has been given the highest sanctity.

However, mythology aside, the feelings between Siegmund and Sieglinde are convincing and command our sympathy, not because Wagner is endorsing an incestuous relationship (in fact the relationship leads to the death of both parties) but because he is describing a loving one. It is the musical expression of their love which is irresistible. In an essay written in Paris when he was twenty-eight, Wagner had this to say:

> What music expresses is eternal, infinite and ideal. It does not express the passion, love or longing of this or that individual in this or that situation, but passion, love, or longing in itself; and this it presents in that unlimited variety of motivations which is the exclusive and particular characteristic of music, foreign and inexpressible in any other language.

Some of Wagner's critics found in the relationship between Siegmund and Sieglinde yet another example of morally reprehensible and socially corrupting tendencies in Wagner's music, tendencies which, in their view, continued scandalously in *Tristan* and culminated morbidly in *Parsifal*. Friedrich Nietzsche, after he had turned against Wagner in the 1870s, declared: 'Is Wagner human at all? Is he not rather a disease? Whatever he touches he infects. He has made music sick ...' An English critic writing in 1882 said: 'We cannot refrain from making a protest against the worship of animal passion which is so striking a feature in the later works of Wagner ... The passion is unholy in itself and its representation is impure ...' So, decadence and immorality were high on the list of objections to Wagner in the late nineteenth century.

During the mid-twentieth century, when Fascism and Communism were at their most prominent and anti-Semitism at its most appalling, the works were shamelessly exploited by the Nazis (with the active collaboration of the widow of Siegfried Wagner), and Hitler's regime depicted them as anti-Semitic and anti-Bolshevist. The opponents of Nazism then damned them precisely on these grounds, swallowing Hitler's propaganda whole.

And what are the objections during our own age? As recently as 1982, one writer, Hartmut Zelinsky, maintained that Wagner had used music as a drug, as an intoxicant, as a philosophy of life. 'This,' he went on, 'is a phenomenon unknown before his time in the history of music and culture. Its consequences were fatal.'

If we accept all of these views, we must conclude that Wagner's music is intoxicating and philosophically unsound as well as unhealthy, immoral, anti-Semitic and anti-Communist. Frankly, this is absurd, and such claims only serve to attract people who, in the past, might have believed that Paganini was in league with the devil and that Lord Byron was 'mad, bad and dangerous to know'.

The reality, of course, is that music, of itself, can no more be good or bad, moral or immoral, than can the spoken word. But it can have a more powerful, even disturbing, effect, because it can by-pass our faculty of reason and tap directly into our emotions and our subconscious mind. Wagner was the supreme exponent of using music to do just that. People who prefer their emotions to remain firmly under the control of their reason are often uncomfortable with Wagner's music, although they might not realise why. Ironically, this can result in apparently rational individuals indulging in the quite irrational objections and associations to which I have referred.

The waters of Wagnerian musical appreciation have, at least in the popular mind, been muddied by the phenomenal amount of (often trivial) material available on his personal life, and on his views on subjects as diverse as vivisection, vegetarianism, hydropathy, institutionalised religion, philosophy, Buddhism, the cultural life of European Jewry, literature, social reform, and nineteenth-century European politics. Towards the end of his life, in despair of developments in Bismarck's Germany, he even contemplated a new life in the United States of America (Minnesota to be precise), comparing its society to that of ancient Athens. His comments and opinions on everything under the sun flew like chips of marble from the sculptor's block. Many were ludicrous;

some were insightful. They were often contradictory. Wagner was not alone in exhibiting personal foibles, and in his voluminous correspondence and other writings he certainly did not attempt to hide them. But no other composer, perhaps no other artist of any kind, has shared his thoughts – wise and foolish, generous and self-centred, open-minded and prejudiced – as he did.

Like other great dramatists – Shakespeare for instance in *King Lear* or Sophocles in *Oedipus The King* – he was concerned to express as powerfully as possible human emotions, strengths, weaknesses and relationships. However, his primary focus was not on the outer world of events but on the inner world of emotions, because this was, in his view, what music could best express. That he was very aware of the distinction is clear in an essay of 1851 entitled *A Communication to My Friends*, in which he wrote: 'The artist addresses himself to Feeling, and not to Understanding. If he is answered in terms of Understanding, then it is quite clear that he has not been understood.'

What about the subjects he chose? What was his intention there? He had something to say about this himself. In 1844, while at work on *Tannhäuser*, he wrote:

> It is not my practice to choose a subject at random, to versify it then think of suitable music to write for it; – if I were to proceed in that way I would be exposed to the difficulty of having to work myself up to a pitch of enthusiasm on two separate occasions, something which is impossible. No, my method of production is different from that: – in the first place I am attracted only by those subjects that reveal themselves to me not only as poetically but, at the same time, as musically significant. And so, even before I set about writing a single line of the text or drafting a scene, I am already thoroughly immersed in the musical aura of my new creation. [2]

In other words, his principal creative stimuli were the emotions prompted by a subject and, in particular, the musical ambience which he associated with those emotions.

Wagner's main source for the story in Act One of *Die Walküre* was the Icelandic *Völsungasaga* (*The Saga of the Volsungs*). He modified and compressed some of the detail but the essentials were retained: Siegmund is descended from Wotan as Volsung was descended from Odin. In both stories the house is built around a tree. The heroine (called Signy in one and Sieglinde in the other) is married against her will, and at her wedding feast an old, one-eyed stranger enters the hall and plunges a sword into the tree trunk, bequeathing it to him who can extract it. Many try to draw the sword from the tree but, in both stories, only Siegmund succeeds. In the *Völsungasaga*, Signy bears her brother's son, as does Sieglinde in *Die Walküre*. The basic plot, therefore, is not really Wagner's at all. He adapted and dramatised an ancient legend, turned it into poetic form and, through music of unprecedented power and beauty, made it interesting to audiences of his time and ours.

If the music of Act One of *Die Walküre* drew inspiration from Wagner's infatuation with Mathilde Wesendonck, Act Two was influenced by a muse of a very different stripe: the philosopher Arthur Schopenhauer. The composition of Act One was finished before the end of August 1854 and, in September that year, Wagner encountered a book which became vastly important to him. It was Schopenhauer's *The World as Will and Idea*. He had, hitherto, been moved philosophically by what he described as the 'cheerful' Greek view of the world, but Schopenhauer's thesis (derived partly from Buddhism), offered the annihilation of the will and complete self-abnegation as the only true means of redemption. This began to occupy his thoughts more and more. Schopenhauer also took the view that music had a privileged place amongst the arts and that it was in music that the 'inner side' of man and also the world in general, found its most profound and complete artistic expression. What music gives us, Schopenhauer had said, is nothing less than the 'secret history of our will', and in melody the constant digressions from and return to the keynote reflects the eternal nature of the human will, which strives, is satisfied, and ever strives anew. Wagner recognised that, instinctively, he had been moving towards a similar conclusion in respect of music. He also saw the relevance of Schopenhauer's view of the world to his Nibelung dramas and, in particular, to the character of Wotan. This then was the springboard from which he continued with the composition of *Die Walküre* late in 1854.

Act Two opens boisterously in a wild, rocky place, inhabited by Wotan and Brünnhilde, the Valkyrie after whom the drama is named. She is his eldest and favourite daughter by the earth goddess Erda. It is an opening filled with agitation, and the theme that we last heard associated with the love of Siegmund and Sieglinde is now burdened with distress. The two lovers are fleeing from Hunding, and Sieglinde in particular is exhausted and overcome with guilt and remorse.

In his earliest drafts for what he at the time called *Siegfrieds Tod* and *Der junge Siegfried*, Wagner had intended to make the young legendary hero the central character of his dramas. However, as his story evolved and *Die Walküre* and *Das Rheingold* were added, it became clear that the central character was really Wotan. All that happens in the *Ring* can, in a sense, be linked to Wotan's needs, his ambitions, his weaknesses and, eventually, his willingness to accept his own end.

Act Two of *Die Walküre* lies at the very heart of *Der Ring des Nibelungen*. It is the fulcrum about which the whole drama turns. It is an Act that requires all of the audience's concentration, because, not only does it place a particular emphasis on the text, but it also contains not one but two dramatic high points: the tormented soliloquy of Wotan as he reveals his innermost anxieties, and the great scene which commences with the annunciation of death by Brünnhilde to Siegmund and ends with her disobedience and fall from grace. These are passages of biblical gravity, and Wagner found their writing a harrowing experience. In November 1854 he wrote to the Princess Sayn-Wittgenstein: 'The subject of the *Valkyrie* affects me far too painfully. There is no grief in the whole world that is not here expressed, most agonisingly. I have been quite ill over it'. In a letter to Liszt in October 1855, he wrote:

> I am worried about the weighty second act: it contains two catastrophes, each so significant and so strong that they really provide content enough for two acts. But the one is so dependent on the other and they follow each other so directly that it was quite impossible to separate them.

When the curtain rises, things are going well for Wotan. He is relishing the idea of the coming battle between Siegmund and Hunding, in which his son is to be victorious. Brünnhilde is instructed to ensure that Siegmund will win and Hunding will die. She launches into her war-cry, a sound so elemental and self-confident that, once heard, it is never forgotten.

Brünnhilde warns Wotan that his wife Fricka is approaching, and his heart sinks: 'The usual storm,' he says gloomily, 'the usual strife'. When Wagner and his second-wife-to-be, Cosima, lived at Tribschen on Lake Lucerne in the 1860s, they kept, amongst other creatures, two peacocks called Wotan and Fricka. No doubt the incessant screeching of these birds reminded them daily of the turbulent married life of the chief of the gods and his consort.

Fricka takes her responsibilities as guardian of marriage very seriously. Her particular crusade on this occasion relates to Wotan's adulterous and incestuous children, and her support for the wronged husband, Hunding. Wotan, rather disingenuously, in view of his involvement in the whole affair, feigns surprise that anyone could take exception to the natural consequences of spring. In his view, the greater crime is a marriage in which there is no love. The parallel with Wagner's own circumstances is obvious.

Wotan urges Fricka to keep an open mind, but she is not to be put off with that sort of talk, and she brings up the subject of Wotan's many infidelities. He ignores these barbs and explains that the gods need a free hero who can achieve their objectives without their intervention, and without even realising that he is assisting them. Fricka argues that, far from being free, Siegmund is merely Wotan himself acting vicariously. Wotan protests that he has not lifted a godly finger to help Siegmund throughout his sad life, to which Fricka replies with devastating logic 'Then do not help him now! Take back the sword.' She demands that, in the battle which is to come, Brünnhilde should protect the wronged husband and let Siegmund die. Wotan is unable to answer these arguments and, in the words of Wagner's stage directions, from this point onwards his whole demeanour expresses an ever-increasing uneasy, profound dejection. A motif which might be labelled 'Wotan's frustration' figures prominently in the orchestra. It derives from the spear motif, symbol of Wotan's will, but it is turned back upon itself with obvious significance. This motif evolves through several other forms as the drama dictates. After Fricka's exit it becomes what might be called the motif of Wotan's revolt, an extreme expression of his frustration. In *Götterdämmerung*, the motif of Wotan's frustration appears in many guises, especially in connection with Hagen's plotting to destroy Siegfried – the ultimate negation of Wotan's will.

Needless to say, Brünnhilde, on her return, is more than a little surprised to discover that her father has changed his mind. However, she is not at all surprised to learn who changed it for him. Eventually he confides in her (indeed he seems to be thinking aloud) that he now despairs of ever freeing himself of the entanglements and treaties which, in the pursuit of power, have been of his own making. He recounts, quietly at first, the story of the theft of the gold and the making of Alberich's ring, his own cunning theft of the ring with Loge's help, Erda's warning, the loss of the ring to Fafner, the birth of Brünnhilde and her eight Valkyrie sisters, the need for a free man to win back the ring, and the threat foretold by Erda of a son born to Alberich. Finally, and bitterly, he instructs Brünnhilde to give victory to Hunding and let Siegmund die. His favourite daughter, who knows him well, cannot believe that he really means this, for he has loved Siegmund. Furiously, and in his frustration, Wotan threatens Brünnhilde with punishment if she disobeys him, and at last she agrees to do what he asks.

This long scene is demanding for an audience, but Wagner considered it the most important scene in the whole *Ring*. Why? because it depicts a complete reversal in Wotan's fortunes and a profound development in his character. By the time it is finished, he has reached the startling conclusion that all he really wants is an end to everything. Wagner, in a letter to August Röckel in 1854, explained what was happening in these terms:

> The course of the drama thus shows the necessity of accepting and giving way to the changeableness, the diversity, the multiplicity, the eternal newness of reality and of life. Wotan rises to the tragic height of willing his own downfall. This is everything that we have to learn from the history of mankind: to will the inevitable and to carry it out oneself.

No wonder that Wagner was so drawn to the philosophy of Schopenhauer when he read *The World as Will and Idea* later that same year.

Wotan storms off, leaving Brünnhilde to direct the course of the battle between Siegmund and Hunding. In the scene which follows, the lovers pause, exhausted in flight, while Hunding's dogs and hunting horns pursue them relentlessly. Sieglinde hallucinates, imagining all kinds of disasters befalling Siegmund and, at last, she drifts into unconsciousness. Then begins the remarkable passage known as the Annunciation of Death.

The music of the doomed lovers is interwoven with that of the destiny to which all human beings must, in the end, yield. Wagner the magician begins casting his spells, which carry us into a sort of waking sleep in which the Valkyrie Brünnhilde appears to Siegmund and tells him of his fate. 'Siegmund,' she says, 'look on me'. Since only those heroes who are about to fall in battle actually see the Valkyries, it is clear that Siegmund's time has come. Siegmund replies that he will gladly go with Brünnhilde as long as Sieglinde can go with him. However, this cannot be. Brünnhilde implores him to give Sieglinde and her unborn child into her care. Defiantly, he refuses to leave his sister-bride and even threatens to slay her while she sleeps if they are to be separated. As Siegmund prepares to kill Sieglinde and himself, the sword motif is heard in the minor key but then transforms itself loudly into an embryonic version of the motif of the unborn Siegfried, reminding us that even more is at stake here than the hapless pair who now await their fate.

Brünnhilde is overcome with compassion for the lovers. She resolves to give victory to Siegmund after all and to risk her father's wrath, knowing that, in doing so, she is carrying out his innermost wish. Sieglinde, in her delirium, relives the destruction of her family home and the murder of her mother. Hunding's voice is heard, battle is joined and Brünnhilde is seen protecting Siegmund. Suddenly Wotan intervenes and extends his spear, on which Siegmund's sword shatters. Hunding drives his spear home and Siegmund falls. No man may continue to live once he has seen a Valkyrie.

Brünnhilde, with fine presence of mind, collects up the broken pieces of the sword, places Sieglinde on her horse and flees the scene. Wotan tells Hunding to inform Fricka that her shame has now been avenged and, with a contemptuous wave of the hand, strikes him dead. Beside himself with rage – and not a little humiliation – Wotan sets out in pursuit of the defiant Valkyrie amidst thunder and lightning. So ends Act Two.

I would hazard a guess that the two pieces of operatic music best known in the world today are both by Wagner. They are the Bridal Chorus from *Lohengrin*, played each week in countless marriage ceremonies from Alaska to Zanzibar, and the Ride of the Valkyries which opens Act Three of *Die Walküre*.

There could hardly be a greater contrast in musical characterisations. In one case, we are in the bridal chamber of the demure and noble Elsa and the shining knight of the unknown name. The music is transparent, gentle and coy. In the other case we are on a wind-swept peak where the wild daughters of Wotan, bearing the corpses of dead warriors, drop from the clouds to rest and regroup *en route* to Valhalla. The Valkyries call to each other, their horses snort and neigh, the wind howls and all the forces of nature are unleashed. The Ride is not subtle, but then neither was the chaos of northern battlefields where the Valkyries appeared, terrifyingly, to dying warriors. It is a *tour de force* of scene-setting and, after the emotionally draining second act, offers a tremendous sense of release and physical excitement. Its theatrical value in this sense is not appreciated when it is torn from its context and played in isolation.

In early Norse mythology, the Valkyries were dark angels of death. It seems that originally, they determined who would live and who would die on the battlefield and in stormy seas. They gathered up chosen heroes to bear them to Odin's (that is Wotan's) glittering Hall of the Slain – *Walhall* – Valhalla. ('Wal' means battlefield.) In later mythology, the Valkyries were romanticised as virginal maidens who waited on the heroes, serving them meat and drink as they waited for the last great battle, called *Ragnarok*, between the gods and the giants; a kind of Armageddon, a twilight of the gods.

Wagner's names for the nine Valkyries have particular meanings. *Brünnhilde*, or Brynhild in Norse mythology, means roughly 'she of the burnished armour'. *Gerhilde* means 'armed with a spear', *Helmwige* 'warrior with a helmet', *Waltraute* 'mighty on the battlefield', *Schwertleite* 'sword wielder', *Ortlinde* 'she whose sword has a flashing point', and *Siegrune* 'she who knows the runes of victory'. Other Valkyries are *Rossweisse* 'riding on a shining horse', and *Grimgerde* 'protected by a helmet'.

What are the warrior maidens calling to each other as they arrive in one's and two's on the rocky peak? To begin with, they are talking about their horses; where to tether them and how to stop them kicking at each other. They exchange information about the dead heroes on their saddles, and blame these former enemies for the unruly behaviour of their mounts. In mythology, the steeds of the Valkyries had probably been suggested by wind-swept rain clouds, and their soaking manes were thought to spray the earth with frost and dew. At last, Brünnhilde arrives in a state of high emotion. Her horse, Grane, has been ridden to exhaustion, and her sisters are astonished to see that she has a woman over her saddle. 'That is no hero!' says Helmwige, foreshadowing Siegfried's startled observation in the last act of *Siegfried*: 'That is no man!' when he uncovers the sleeping Brünnhilde.

In their anxiety to learn more of Brünnhilde's plight, her sisters all speak at once, just as people do in such circumstances. This gives Wagner an opportunity to display his mastery of ensemble writing, of which there has been practically none so far in *The Ring*. Four and then eight vocal lines are handled simultaneously to create an effect of agitation and concern. These examples of polyphonic writing remind us that, even though Wagner was a great champion of new developments in music (his oft-quoted injunction to others was 'create something new!') he was a master of old forms as well.

We saw in *Das Rheingold* how he put new wine in old bottles, so to speak, in the scene in Nibelheim, where a complicated series of events was given unity and form along the lines of an extended rondo. In *Die Meistersinger von Nürnberg*, that sublime comedy of his maturity (which was written, along with *Tristan*, during a twelve year break between Acts Two and Three of *Siegfried*), he showed what could still be done with the chorale and the fugue. But, in all of these cases, the old forms were harnessed for particular dramatic purposes. So, for example, the chorale gives us an image of the worthy citizens of post-Reformation Nuremberg, and the fugue gives musical expression to a street brawl.

In his adult life, Wagner came to revere J.S. Bach. Wagner had been born in Leipzig and was baptised in the Thomaskirche, at which Bach had been Cantor. Bach had spent the latter half of his life in Leipzig until his death in 1750, and Wagner spent his early life there, including a short and colourful time at the University. Theodor Weinlig was one of Bach's successors at St Thomas's, and Wagner became Weinlig's pupil at the age of eighteen, in 1831. After a nearly disastrous beginning to their relationship, the months which they spent together as pupil and master became one of the happiest periods in Wagner's life. He drew on his memories of it in *Die Meistersinger*, in which Hans Sachs advises the impetuous young Walther not to reject the old in his rush to embrace the new. Most importantly, it was from Weinlig that the young Richard learnt the art of the fugue. In his autobiography, *Mein Leben*, he describes what happened in the following way:

> The joint work on fugues became the basis for the most productive affection between me and my genial teacher, for we both enjoyed such tasks immensely. I was amazed to see how quickly the time flew. In eight weeks I had not only gone through a number of the most intricate fugues but had also waded quickly through the most difficult contrapuntal exercises, when one day, after I had handed him an extremely elaborate double fugue, he took my breath away

by telling me I should have the piece framed because he had nothing more to teach me... One of the most important results of his influence on me was the satisfaction I now found in clarity and fluidity, which he had taught me to value by his own example. Even when he gave me that first fugal exercise, I had had to write proper vocal parts for it with the words written in below the stave; my feeling for vocal writing had been awakened in this manner.

According to Cosima's diaries, Wagner considered the 48 Preludes and Fugues of *The Well-tempered Clavier* and the Motets the most consummate of Bach's works. There are many references in the diaries to the Preludes and Fugues, to Wagner's playing of them and his comments on this one or that. For example: in December 1877, he says of one:

That gave me my direction. It is incredible how many things in music passed me by without leaving any impression, but that made me what I am. It is immortal! No one else has ever done anything like it!

Again, in 1878:

In him (Bach) you find all the seeds which later flourished in so fertile a soil as Beethoven's imagination; much of what Bach wrote down was done unconsciously, as if in a dream; my 'unending melody' is predestined in it.

If you think it strange to speak of Bach's *Well-tempered Clavier*, and Wotan's hysterical daughters in the same breath, then consider this. Bach's compositions, quite frequently, utilised extra-musical ideas derived from textural references. Albert Schweitzer catalogued many examples which, by their form, rhythm, or harmonic structure described actions such as walking or falling, natural phenomena such as waves or clouds, and emotions such as terror, grief and joy. So for example, in the aria *'Come, healing cross'* in the *St Matthew Passion*, the viola da gamba obbligato, with its quadruple stopping and dotted rhythm, provides a pictorial representation of the effort involved in lifting and dragging a heavy cross. In one Cantata, which uses Christ's words 'It is expedient for you that I go away. For if I go not away, the Comforter will not come unto you', Bach gives to the basses a 'walking' motif, while, to use Schweitzer's words, the noble arabesque of the oboe above it expresses sublime consolation.

Keep this in mind when you listen to the scene in Act Three of *Die Walküre*, in which the eight Valkyries express their dismay at Wotan's decision to punish Brünnhilde. The punishment, which has just been announced, is that Brünnhilde will be put to sleep on the rock where they are standing. She will be left as a mortal woman, to be claimed by the first man who comes along and awakens her. The Valkyries plead with their father not to enforce such a punishment, and lament the shame of Brünnhilde's having to submit to the will of a man. We hear the eight pleading voices in counterpoint and then, as if to describe the object of their fears, the orchestra projects over the vocal parts a striking vision of a stranger joyfully encountering the sleeping Brünnhilde and claiming her for his own. All of this is accomplished in just half a minute, but it fits seamlessly into the dramatic context and is a good example of Wagner's contrapuntal technique, first acquired under the guiding hand of Master Weinlig of the Thomaskirche in Leipzig.

But we are getting ahead of ourselves. Before Wotan arrives in search of Brünnhilde, a highly charged scene has been taking place involving Sieglinde. She has arrived with Brünnhilde, traumatised and exhausted by her flight from Hunding and shocked by the sudden death of Siegmund. Brünnhilde herself has just witnessed the fearsome anger of her father and has fled in panic. She pleads with her sisters to lend her a fresh horse but they tell her it would be of no use. There can be no escape from Wotan. Sieglinde overhears the various exchanges and says that she should have been left to die at the side of Siegmund. However, when Brünnhilde urges her to live for the sake of the Volsung who grows in her womb, Sieglinde is at first terrified but then becomes elated with the thought that she is carrying Siegmund's child. Now she asks the Valkyries to save her unborn child and to shelter them both.

Only Brünnhilde is willing, once more, to put herself at risk. She will stand and face Wotan's wrath while Sieglinde escapes on foot to the east. In the east, her sisters report, there is a great forest in which Fafner, now in the form of a dragon, guards the Nibelung hoard and Alberich's ring. Wotan avoids going there. In German mythology, the east often carries a connotation of being mysterious and forbidding, a place of magic and danger. Brünnhilde urges Sieglinde to endure the hard life which will be her lot, for the sake of the noblest of heroes whom she carries within her. She gives Sieglinde the fragments of the sword that was shattered on Wotan's spear. Your son shall forge it anew, says Brünnhilde, and he shall be called Siegfried – which means 'peace through victory'.

If Brünnhilde's appearance to the doomed Siegmund in Act Two was an annunciation of death, her message to Sieglinde in Act Three must surely be an annunciation of life. There is an obvious parallel with the angel's annunciation to the Virgin Mary that she will bear a son and shall call him Jesus. This is hardly a coincidence. Siegfried will be a hero in a legendary sense because he will be fearless, kill the dragon and win the ring. But he is already a hero or, if you like, a deliverer, in a philosophical sense, in that he symbolises hope and life amidst hopelessness and decay – another analogy with Christ. And incidentally, in 1849, one year after writing his prose sketch for a Nibelung drama, Wagner sketched out a five act tragedy called *Jesus of Nazareth*. Nothing came of this, but it is not too fanciful to see how aspects of the Gospel story might have fertilised his poetic treatment of the story of Siegfried. The poem (as he called the libretto) of *Die*

Walküre was written only a couple of years later. At the mention of her son's name, Sieglinde's spirits soar ecstatically. *O hehrstes Wunder!* – O sublime miracle! – she sings, and proceeds with her own Magnificat, praising Brünnhilde for being the bearer of such news, and vowing to save the infant 'for him whom we loved' that is, for Siegmund. The motif which expresses the words *O hehrstes Wunder!* is traditionally known by the title 'Redemption through Love'. There might be better ways to describe it,[3] but this title does reflect an important implication of the motif, namely that hope and love will survive when all else has gone. We hear this motif for the first time with Sieglinde's words, and we shall hear it only once more, in the closing bars of *Götterdämmerung*. It will become the very last musical idea of *The Ring*.

Apart from its highly effective dramatic qualities, which are heightened because it is used so sparingly, the Redemption through Love motif is interesting in that the vocal line uses a melodic phrase of six notes for just two syllables, which is unusual for Wagner. The idea of mangling a word to fit a pre-determined musical phrase, (*à la* Handel for example) was anathema to him. However, once again, Wagner was prepared to break his own rules and hark back to earlier practices in the interests of the drama. This happens again in the final scene of *Siegfried* when Brünnhilde rhapsodises with the unusually extended melody which is also heard at the beginning of the *Siegfried Idyll*. Ecstasy, rhapsody, delirium: all seem to warrant this kind of treatment in Wagner's mind. Heard in isolation, Sieglinde's music is glorious enough, but in the context of all that has gone before – anxiety and despair, death and hopelessness – it is positively electrifying.

Sieglinde has left the scene by the time Wotan arrives, bristling with anger. We sense that Brünnhilde's disobedience is only part of the reason for his black mood. Below the surface he is also angry at having opened himself to humiliation by Fricka.

He knows all too well that his favourite daughter was doing what he really wanted to do, but was prevented from doing. In lashing out at Brünnhilde therefore, he is also punishing himself. And what punishment he metes out! He lists the ways in which he had depended on her before her disobedience, and he says that never again will he ask her to do anything for him. She will be a Valkyrie no more. He condemns her to mortality and to the ignominy of being claimed by the first man who chances by. We have not heard anything like this since Alberich's curse in the fourth scene of *Das Rheingold*.

After her initial shock at the extent of her father's rejection, Brünnhilde begins a quiet appeal to the feelings of love and compassion which she knows are still buried deep inside him. She is on strong ground in reminding him of what was really in his heart: his feelings of love for his son. He acknowledges that, in his words, cruel fate had forbidden what he had longed to do. Brünnhilde tells him that she would rather he strike her dead with his spear than have to submit to his intended punishment. But if she must be locked in sleep, she says, if she must become a mortal woman and succumb to the first man who finds her, then let that man be fearless and free. 'At your command,' she adds, 'a flame can be kindled, a fiery guardian girding the rock, which will lick with its tongues and tear with its teeth any craven who dares to approach'. As Wotan's rage subsides and compassion returns to his heart, he finally agrees. 'Farewell, my valiant, glorious child!' he says. 'You were the holiest pride of my heart. Farewell! Farewell!

Then begins one of the most moving and wonderful parts of the whole *Ring*. Wotan promises to encircle the Valkyrie's rock with fire: '... one alone wins you as bride,' he says, 'one freer than I, the god.' Page after page of words and music is filled with tender expressions of paternal love. Gone is the wrathful god; in his place now is a protecting father. He kisses her gently on the eyes, and slumber gradually overtakes her. He lays her on a mossy bank, closes her helmet and covers her with her shield. The orchestra passes through successive veils of chromaticism and we feel the magic of sleep descending and enveloping the whole scene. The slumber motif gently rises and falls, like the rise and fall of breathing in the midst of sleep. Wotan says nothing for quite a long time, the orchestra expressing feelings which are too deep for words.

The slumber motif is one of those miraculous themes which Wagner was able to produce on cue to convey the essence of the drama. It depends for its effect both on its particular shape and on its tempo, which needs to be broad and peaceful.

Wagner was one of the fathers of modern conducting, and he attached the greatest importance to correct tempo. This was not tempo determined in a mechanical and inflexible way, but tempo which came naturally out of what he called the *melos*, the melodic soul of a scene, a movement, a section, a phrase, even an individual bar. Time and again he lamented the fact that few conductors of his day could appreciate why one tempo was right and another was wrong. His comments on finding the right tempo are quite illuminating and they are still a useful guide for conductors, whether in the concert hall or the opera house.

In an essay on conducting written in 1869, he said:

> I furnished my earlier operas ... with eloquent directions for tempo, and fixed them past mistaking (so I thought) by metronomic ciphers. But whenever I heard a foolish tempo in a performance of my *Tannhäuser*, for instance, my recriminations were always parried by the plea that my metronomic marks had been followed most scrupulously. So I saw how uncertain must be the value of mathematics in music, and thenceforth dispensed with the metronome; contenting myself with quite general indications for the principal time measure and devoting all my forethought to its modifications, since our conductors know as good as nothing of the latter.

He quoted Mendelssohn who, he said, had told him that 'a too slow tempo was the devil, and for choice he would rather things were taken too fast'. Mendelssohn had suggested that 'a really good rendering was a rarity at any time; with a little care, however, one might gloss things over; and this could best be done by never dawdling, but covering the ground at a good stiff pace'. During a visit to London in 1855, to conduct concerts for the Philharmonic Society, Wagner discovered that this Mendelssohnian dictum had been raised to the status of a tradition.

> In fact it so well suited the customs and peculiarities of this Society's concerts that it almost seemed as if Mendelssohn had derived his mode of rendering from them. A huge amount of music was consumed at those concerts, but only one rehearsal allowed for each performance ... The thing flowed on like water from a public fountain; to attempt to check it was out of the question, and every allegro ended as an indisputable presto. [4]

Soon after the final performance of the *Ring* in 1876, Wagner wrote to a friend:

> I simply do not know any conductor I could trust to perform my music in the right way, or any actor-singer of whom I could expect a proper realisation of my dramatic sense unless I myself had taught him everything, measure by measure, phrase by phrase. The German capacity for bungling in every sphere of art is unique: it reduces me to the condition in which you found me after the last *Götterdämmerung*. What horrified me was the discovery that my conductor, Hans Richter, whom nevertheless I regard as the best I know, often could not maintain the right tempo even when he had found it, simply because he was incapable of understanding why it should be thus and not otherwise.

The final scene of *Die Walküre* is filled with a serenity and inevitability which sets it apart from everything else in *The Ring*. It also creates a mood of suspended animation. We have reached an end point, but it is not *the* end. More will happen, but nothing will be the same again. Wotan's reverie is broken by his sudden realisation that he must summon Loge, or at least his element, to encircle Brünnhilde with a fiery moat. This will be his last positive act and will fix irrevocably his own destiny. The stern, descending spear motif, symbol of his authority, signals his resolve. Three time he strikes a rock with his spear, in a gesture which is reminiscent of Moses striking a rock in the desert to bring forth water for the children of Israel.

What happens next is best left for the music alone to describe, and for our mind's eye to imagine. As Wagner's grandson, Wieland, put it, it is well-nigh impossible to duplicate for the eye what the orchestra is conveying so triumphantly to our ears. A flame leaps from the rock and gradually increases to an ever-brightening fiery glow. Flickering flames appear and bright shooting flames surround Wotan. With his spear, he directs the sea of fire to encircle the rock, from where it spreads to enclose the whole mountain. 'Only the man who braves my spear-point' he says 'can pass through this sea of flame!', and the motif of the unborn Siegfried makes its presence felt in the orchestra. With one last, sorrowful look back at the sleeping Brünnhilde, Wotan disappears through the fire.

After his separation from Brünnhilde, Wotan is no more than a departed spirit. Now he can only accept things; let things happen as they must. It is left to Siegfried – the man of free will, who knows that death is preferable to living in fear – to brave Wotan's spear point and pass through the fire. But these are matters for the future. For the moment, we are conscious only of the glorious music of the magic fire and Brünnhilde's sleep and, surprisingly, of a passing reference to the annunciation of death. Brünnhilde will still live, but now she is as dead to Wotan as is the hapless Siegmund.

When the fire music takes hold of the orchestra completely, the curtain falls.

Siegfried reforges Siegmund's sword, Notung.
Twelfth-century woodcarving.

Siegfried

'He is small and bent, somewhat deformed and hobbling. His head is abnormally large, his face a dark ashen colour and wrinkled, his eyes small and piercing, with red rims, his grey beard long and scrubby, his head is bald and covered with a red cap. He wears a dark grey smock with a broad belt about his loins: feet bare, with thick coarse soles underneath.' No, this is not Siegfried! It is Mime, the Nibelung, whom we last saw in *Das Rheingold*, howling pitifully at the bullying of his brother Alberich. This description appears in the original stage directions of *Der junge Siegfried* which Wagner had written in 1851 as a lighter prologue to the tragedy of *Siegfrieds Tod*.

The description is not retained in the final version of the work, but it is reflected in what Siegfried himself has to say in the first scene: 'I only have to look at you to see that you're evil in all that you do. When I watch you standing about, shuffling and nodding, twitching and slinking and blinking your eyes, I'd like to seize you by your nodding neck and put an end to your loathsome blinking!' Hardly a kindly attitude towards a guardian one might think, but then, Mime harbours similar feelings towards Siegfried, although he keeps these very much to himself. 'From the sap of plants,' thinks Mime, 'I'll make a potent brew. If he tastes just one drop he'll fall asleep. I'll seize the sword and dispatch him easily; then the ring and the gold will be mine.'

Where else would one find such vivid statements of greed and mutual mistrust, such devious scheming and bloodthirsty intent, such an association of evil with the strange and the ugly? The answer, quite plainly, is in children's fairy-tales and, especially, the tales collected by the brothers Grimm.

Grimms' *Fairy-Tales* or, more correctly, *Children's and Household Tales* by Wilhelm and Jakob Grimm, as well as Wilhelm Grimm's *German Book of Heroes*, held a great fascination for Wagner. Indeed, in the late 1840s, he told a friend that he would write no more grand operas but only fairy tales.[1] I referred earlier to his inspiration in 1851 to combine the legend of Siegfried, derived from *Das Nibelungenlied* and the earlier *Poetic Edda*, with the *Story of the Youth Who Went Forth to Learn What Fear Was*. Acts One and Two of *Siegfried* are pure fairy-tale. Consider the ingredients. The location is a dark forest. We see, in turn, an evil dwarf, a handsome youth who does not know fear, a bear, an ominous stranger who calls himself the Wanderer, a second evil dwarf who is the brother of the first, a talking dragon and a talking bird. In Act Three there is also a beautiful maiden who is awakened from a long sleep by a kiss from the handsome youth who passes through a wall of fire to reach her.

Fairy-tales, as works of art, serve the purpose of informing us that life involves dangerous struggles, and that only by mastering crises and confronting fears can we eventually find our true selves. That is why frightening and unpleasant things often happen in them. Furthermore, the image of a man in a dark, impenetrable forest is an ancient literary symbol for the search for self-knowledge, for the resolution of a moral crisis or the overcoming of some obstacle to self-confidence. Dante, for example, uses such an image at the beginning of *The Divine Comedy*. The darkness of the forest is a projection of a darkness within the character himself. By overcoming these obstacles the character wins a moral victory over his own weaknesses.

One of the best known of the Grimms' fairy-tales, that of *Hänsel und Gretel*, illustrates the role of negative characters in helping the positive characters to grow in self-knowledge and self-reliance. Consider this passage, which seems particularly relevant to Act One of *Siegfried*:

> The old woman had only pretended to be kind, but she was in reality a wicked witch, who lay in wait for children and had only built a house of bread in order to entice them there. When a child fell into her power, she killed it, cooked and ate it, and that was a feast day for her. Witches have red eyes, and cannot see far, but they have a keen sense of smell like the beasts, and know when human beings draw near. [2]

We know that Gretel saved her brother by pushing the witch into her own oven. Because the children were able to gain control of their nightmare – made tangible in the form of the witch – they gained confidence in their own abilities to defeat evil and rescue themselves. So it is with Siegfried, although he is in such a state of ignorance or, if you like, innocence, that he does not even realise that he should be afraid of the dangers which confront him.

We have moved into a dramatic world that is very different from what has gone before. I have described *Das Rheingold* as a kind of morality play, in which the world's innocence is lost to greed and a lust for power and wealth. Different again is *Die Walküre*, the first day of Wagner's Festival Drama, which is full of human warmth and introspection, illuminated by occasional flashes of passion and tragedy. In it we witness the rapid decline of Wotan from a position of power and confidence to one of impotence and dejection. We also witness the growth of Brünnhilde from a devoted daughter to a noble individual, motivated by love and compassion. Then comes the fairy-tale of *Siegfried*. Like *Rheingold*, it is an allegory of the human condition, but the focus this time is not on venality but on vulnerability – both male and female.

Because Wagner wrote the poems of the four dramas in reverse order, he had to revisit the earlier texts and make adjustments to accommodate events which, although written later, occurred earlier in the narrative. He described this process in his autobiography.

> I wrote the poem of *Das Rheingold* in October and November of that year [that is 1852], whereby I brought the whole cycle of my Nibelung dramas to completion in reverse order. At the same time I revised *Der junge Siegfried* and especially *Siegfrieds Tod* in such a way that they now related correctly to the whole, and this last work in particular was considerably expanded to reflect the palpable significance of the entire drama. Accordingly, I had to give this final drama in the cycle a new title that would correspond to this altered relationship. I called it *Götterdämmerung*, while I changed *Der junge Siegfried*, inasmuch as this work no longer represented merely an isolated episode in the life of its hero but rather showed him in relationship to the other principal characters of the dramas, simply to *Siegfried*.

The young hero is an innocent abroad in a very dangerous and unsympathetic world. He is probably about seventeen when we first encounter him. After Sieglinde died giving birth, he was raised by Mime in the depths of the forest. Mime is a much weaker character than his brother Alberich, and has to resort to wiles and stratagems to get his way. What amazing good fortune, he would have thought, to have come across a scion of the Volsung race in the form of a frail, orphaned baby. Now, at last, he would get even with his bullying brother. He would train Siegfried to win for him Alberich's ring and the golden hoard which Fafner, the giant turned dragon, guards in his forest lair. And after that?

Well, Siegfried would have served his purpose. There would be no place for him in Mime's new world, a world in which Mime would be king!

But what of Siegfried's world? It is important to remember that Siegfried has not met, nor has he even seen, another person – male or female – other than Mime the Nibelung. All that he knows has been learnt from his evil guardian and from observing the forest creatures. He is, in every sense, a child of nature.

Consider this drama from Siegfried's perspective, a perspective dominated by physical experiences and by the corrupting tutelage, the bad influence, of Mime. To a large degree, Siegfried is a product of the forest and of his five senses. That is why he feels a kinship with his friend the bear, the birds of the air, the fish of the streams, and even the gentle doe which he associates instinctively with his unknown mother. Wagner draws attention to this sensory world through the 'texture' of instrumental sounds, the melodious evocations of nature, the clash and clang, heat and steam of Mime's forge, the taste of Fafner's blood, the flickering, menacing lights of the forest, the dazzling sunlight of the mountain top, even the 'warm, fragrant breath' of the sleeping Brünnhilde. However, nature is evoked not just for its own sake.

It seems to me that in this work, more than in any other, Wagner uses the physical environment as a metaphor for psychological influences and relationships. In true fairy-tale fashion, the physical ugliness of Mime is taken to be an outward and visible sign of his evil intentions. The benign aspect of the forest, with its rustling leaves and bird songs, is more of a real home to Siegfried than Mime's bleak cave, or anything else he knows. Little wonder then that, in Act Two, it is within the comforting embrace of a linden tree and the womb-like sounds of the Forest Murmurs, that his thoughts turn to the mother for whom he longs, and he wonders what she was like. 'Must every human mother die when a child is born?' he asks himself. How sad the world would be then.

Throughout this marvellous work, the orchestra paints not only the changing physical environment (which it does with unsurpassed eloquence) but also the changing moods and hidden feelings of the characters. We cross from the physical world to a metaphysical one when we hear the dragon and the Woodbird speaking. This doesn't happen in any of the other dramas. The rams that draw Fricka's chariot don't speak, nor does Brünnhilde's horse nor Wotan's ravens (which makes them easy to dispense with in modern productions).

The dragon and the bird speak in *Siegfried* because we are in the realm of sign and symbol, allegory and illusion. We even hear the secret thoughts of Mime, as he tries to mask his murderous intentions with hypocrisy and guile. Appearances conceal hidden meanings; symbolism is everywhere; nothing is what it seems. The shattering of Wotan's spear by the sword *Notung* in Act Three, reversing the order of events in *Die Walküre*, signifies Wotan's irrelevance and makes it plain that the future belongs to Siegfried. The fire through which Siegfried passes in order to awaken Brünnhilde symbolises the last of the trials he must undergo in order to fulfil his destiny.

There is an obvious parallel here with the Grimms' fairy-tale of *Briar-Rose*, better known to us as *The Sleeping Beauty*, in which the prince must pass through a wall of briars to awaken the princess with a kiss. There is also a similarity with Mozart's *Die Zauberflöte*, a work which Wagner admired greatly. In that opera, Tamino must undergo an ordeal by fire in order to overcome fear of death and enter the temple with Pamina. The awakening of Brünnhilde marks the point at which the adolescent Siegfried becomes a man. It is his initiation rite, for it is through his discovery of woman that he learns fear and passion at the same time. Thus, from Act Three of *Siegfried* onwards, both Siegfried and Brünnhilde are transformed. They begin new lives, both as individuals and together.

Wagner had several reasons for interrupting work on *The Ring* at the end of Act Two of *Siegfried*, but it was a logical point at which to leave behind the allegorical atmosphere of the forest with its implications of childish innocence, and begin a transition to the tremendous new sound world of *Götterdämmerung*. Before this could happen, he would write two utterly contrasting masterpieces, *Tristan und Isolde* and *Die Meistersinger von Nürnberg*.

Let us go back to the beginning of Act One. Before the curtain rises, we hear the soft and ominous roll of a kettledrum, to which is added an equally soft scheming motif low on the bassoons. Somebody is pondering something, but who and what? Other motifs soon provide an answer. We hear the rhythmic sound of a smith's hammer on an anvil, familiar to us from the Nibelheim scene in *Das Rheingold*, and a curious 'limping' musical figure involving three grace notes and a falling note, suggestive of deviousness and malign intent. This motif is associated with the Nibelung, Mime. When the ring motif is added shortly afterwards, we are left in no doubt as to the object of Mime's scheming. So, the picture is complete even before the stage is revealed to us.

When the curtain rises, sure enough, there is Mime tapping away at a sword blade, to which he is putting the finishing touches. He complains that every time he makes a sword, the insolent boy Siegfried just laughs and snaps it in half. Only the sword *Notung* would be strong enough to withstand this rough handling, but there is no way that he can weld its fragments together. In the course of his monologue he reveals that he intends to use Siegfried to kill Fafner and obtain the ring.

While Mime is still complaining to himself, Siegfried's boisterous call is heard and he runs in, driving before him a great shambling forest bear. The double-basses growl in a bear-like manner as the beast heads towards the Nibelung. Mime is frightened out of his wits and hides behind the anvil until the laughing Siegfried has had enough of his childish pranks and drives the bear out into the forest again. This lively interlude is typical of teenage mischief, but it is more than that. It demonstrates, early in the piece, Siegfried's complete absence of fear, and his naivety. After all, a fully grown bear is a dangerous creature which might just as easily turn on the boy as on Mime. It also points up Mime's extreme nervousness, and shows that although Siegfried is just a boy, his physical strength and exuberance make him more than a match for the dwarfish Mime, who has to resort to cunning in order to get his way.

Siegfried, as a character, has had rather a bad press in modern times, especially since the Second World War. The popular parody, which is usually conjured up by people who know nothing about the *Ring*, is of some Teutonic super-hero with nasty habits and more brawn than brain. The fact is that, despite all the references to heroic expectations, the only heroic thing that Siegfried does is to pass through the wall of fire that encircles Brünnhilde's rock. He saves no one from danger and changes nothing for the better, and even when he kills the dragon he uses a magic sword and is insensitive to any risk.

He does not understand what the fuss over the ring is all about and he certainly does not attempt to use the ring, other than as a token of his love for Brünnhilde. He is deceived, drugged, betrayed and eventually murdered. Some hero! No, in practice, Siegfried is just an innocent abroad, a symbol of hope in a hopeless world, who is caught up in machinations he does not comprehend, just as the innocent Prince Tamino was caught up in the machinations of the Queen of the Night and Sarastro. Siegfried becomes a tragic figure. The hope which is vested in him never bears fruit and he falls victim to an evil which he barely understands. That is why his funeral music is filled with such poignancy. So much promise is cut short and remains unfulfilled. We can identify with this even in our modern world. Every time we hear of a promising young life snuffed out by a senseless killing, a tragic accident or the brutality of war, we can appreciate what Siegfried really stands for in *Der Ring des Nibelungen*.

Wagner himself was appalled by thoughts of the waste of young life, so often associated with the collapse of an old political order. He was especially sensitive to this after the birth of his own son, whom he named Siegfried. He had personally witnessed the killing of students and other revolutionaries by the Saxon and Prussian authorities during the Dresden uprisings of 1849. He shared the strong folk memories of invasions, firstly by the armies of Louis XIV who had attacked the decaying Holy Roman Empire in the 1680s, then by French revolutionary armies who had annexed German cities west of the Rhine in 1792, and then by Napoleon's armies between 1804 and 1806, also preying on the remains of the old Empire. Inevitably, it seemed, the passing of one era and the birth of another was attended by tragedy and the sacrifice of the young.

It is not easy to convey Siegfried's youthful vulnerability on the stage, because only singers of experience and stamina can do justice to this most demanding of roles; and they seldom resemble athletic teenage boys! It also takes a while to warm to Siegfried as a character. He is ill-mannered, breaks swords that have taken a long time to make, tips over food that has been prepared for him, and sets a wild animal on his guardian. His attitude towards Mime is one of unmitigated hostility.

For his part, the wizened dwarf whines on and on about how much he has done for the boy and the sacrifices he has made. He keeps this up while he is preparing a meal, and the orchestra follows his domestic activities with an entertaining commentary on cooking; violas and cellos using the wooden parts of their bows, and low clarinets bubbling their amusement. Despite Mime's best efforts to make Siegfried feel guilty for his ingratitude, the boy continues his torrent of abuse. He says that the only thing Mime hasn't been able to teach him is how not to loathe the sight of him! Indeed, he is so repelled by him that he doesn't know why he keeps returning to the cave. Mime suggests that this must be because, deep down, he is dear to Siegfried's heart. This makes the boy laugh. 'Have you forgotten that I can't bear the sight of you?' he says. Mime replies that he must learn to tame his wild feelings. All creatures return to their parents because they love them. This invites the obvious question from Siegfried – then where is Mime's wife? Where is his own mother? Mime is rather embarrassed by this line of questioning and replies desperately that he is father and mother in one. Siegfried doesn't believe this for a moment. He has observed the creatures of the forest and has seen how the young resemble their parents. He knows from his own reflection in a stream that he does not resemble Mime any more than a silvery fish resembles a toad. 'And no fish had a toad for a father!' he says. Siegfried then realises why it is that he keeps returning to Mime: because Mime alone can tell him about his father and mother.

At first, the dwarf pretends that he doesn't understand what the boy is talking about. 'What father! What mother! Meaningless questions!' he exclaims. Siegfried then grabs him by the throat and shakes him until Mime gestures that he will tell him everything. And so he begins his account of how, in the woods, he found a woman who lay and wept. She gave birth, a birth cruel and painful. She died but Siegfried was born. 'My mother died because of me?' says Siegfried quietly. Mime reveals that her name was Sieglinde, but he pretends not to know the name of his father, revealing only that he fell in battle. The boy asks for proof that all of this is true, and Mime produces the shattered pieces of the sword *Notung*. Elated by the discovery of his father's sword, Siegfried instructs Mime to repair it as quickly as possible so that, at last, he can leave the miserable cave and roam freely through the world. He can barely contain his delight: 'As the fish swims through the waters, as the finch flies through the branches, so shall I fly far away with the wind through the woods; then Mime, I shall never see you again!' He rushes out into the forest with Mime shouting after him.

Mime is now faced with a dilemma. If Siegfried leaves him he will lose his opportunity to win the ring from the dragon Fafner. But he also knows that without *Notung*, Siegfried will not be equipped to confront Fafner. While Mime is pondering this predicament, crouching behind the anvil, Wotan in the guise of the Wanderer enters the cave from the forest.

The Wanderer greets Mime courteously: 'Hail, worthy smith!' He introduces himself as a weary traveller who would rest awhile by Mime's hearth. Mime is irritated by this interruption and his attitude is cool, to say the least. He suggests that the Wanderer might like to keep on wandering. The visitor asks if Mime would like to learn something from him and hints that ill fortune attends those who withhold their hospitality. He offers to wager his own head in trying to answer any three questions put to him.

Mime succumbs to the invitation and asks three simple questions about the roles of the Nibelungs, the giants and the gods in the cosmic order of things; all of which are easily answered. When the Wanderer speaks of the gods, his spear point touches the ground and distant thunder is heard, much to Mime's alarm. Then, to Mime's continuing distress, the Wanderer asks him three questions on forfeit of his head. He asks about the race whom Wotan loves above all others but has treated harshly – the Volsungs. He asks the name of the sword which Siegfried must use if he is to kill Fafner – *Notung*. So far so good for Mime.

The question-and-answer game serves to remind us of events in earlier dramas and to reinforce story lines and musical motifs. However, it also reveals how the narrator (in this case Wotan) views past events. One new piece of information emerges about Wotan's perceptions. He refers to Alberich as 'Black Alberich' and himself, Wotan, as 'Light Alberich'. In other words, he acknowledges that they are two of a kind, two sides of the one coin, two aspects of the one persona.

The Wanderer's last question is: who shall forge *Notung* anew? This sends Mime into paroxysms of fear because, quite frankly, he doesn't know and foolishly had not used one of his questions to find out. The answer is revealed: 'One who has never learnt fear'. The Wanderer advises Mime to guard his head well and leaves it forfeit to him who does not know fear. He then departs as mysteriously as he came.

If Mime thought he was in trouble before, that was nothing compared to the mess in which he now finds himself. Put simply, if Siegfried learns about fear he is unlikely to confront Fafner. But if he remains ignorant of fear, then it will be to him that Mime's head will be forfeit. It is all too much for Mime and he begins to hallucinate. He sees flickering lights in the forest, hears strange noises and imagines the gaping maw of a monster about to devour him. It is Fafner! Fafner!

This fascinating outburst is a kind of waking nightmare, which the orchestra describes in graphic detail. The slumber motif, which conveyed such peace and calm at the end of *Die Walküre*, is now twisted and distorted, its harmonies stretched out of recognition. The full descriptive palette of the Wagnerian orchestra is used to evoke the nightmarish vision which reduces Mime to a quivering heap behind his anvil.

The orchestral richness of *Siegfried* is one of its particular glories. In this work, Wagner uses instrumental tone colour as never before, to create and then change a mood with powerful effect. The late John Culshaw, producer of the celebrated Decca recording of the 1960s, observed that it takes time to play even a simple melody or to establish an harmonic progression; but a subtle, unexpected change in instrumental colour can alter a mood in an instant.

Wagner was very particular about the structure of his orchestra and the use to which its instruments were put. He was one of the greatest orchestrators of any period, as other composers have been quick to acknowledge. Richard Strauss, for example, recommended that the student of orchestration should compare Wagner's eleven scores with each other, and note how each has its own combination of instruments, its own orchestral style, and how each says what it wants to say in the simplest way, with moderation in the use of means.

Contrary to what many people believe, Wagner's use of the orchestra does exhibit great restraint and the most careful judgment. His orchestra was large, but this was to give him a wider variety of tonal colours and textures from which to draw, not to give a bigger sound overall, although that might at times be a consequence. Wagner's approach to the orchestra was reflected in his comment that it was 'no mere compost of washy tone ingredients but consisted of a rich association of instruments with unbounded power of adding to its numbers'. In his words, each instrument has a definite individuality and clothes the tone produced with an equally individual garment. Conductor Jeffrey Tate has commented that Wagner's very sparing use of his huge orchestra is astonishing, and he has described the *Ring* as a whole, as one of the most intensely beautiful creations of the European tradition.

With many composers it is possible to take, say, an aria or ensemble or orchestral interlude from one of their works and insert it, virtually unchanged, into another, without the average listener being any the wiser. Some quite famous composers made a regular practice of doing just that! Their approach was 'when you're on a good thing, repeat it'. But this would be quite impossible with Wagner's music, because each of his works exists in its own distinctive sound world. Almost every bar belongs to a unique emotional environment – the silvery, dream-like world of *Lohengrin*, the atonal eroticism of *Tristan*, the mellow confidence and good-humour of *Meistersinger*, and *Parsifal*, at once mystical and sensual, whose colours, said Debussy, seemed to be 'illuminated as from behind'.

And then, of course, there are the four parts of the *Ring*, each of which has as much in common with the others as it has differences in mood and purpose. Interestingly, Wagner does quote himself in one of his works, just as Mozart quotes *Figaro* in the last scene of *Don Giovanni*. In Act Three of *Die Meistersinger*, Hans Sachs refers in a few lines to the sad tale of *Tristan und Isolde*, and the orchestra, in an instant, takes on the distinctive harmonies and colouring of that tragic story of love and longing. There is no way that this insertion could pass unnoticed, even by those who did not understand a word of what was being sung.

Berlioz, who was a master of instrumentation and wrote a famous handbook on the subject, referred particularly to the extraordinary effects created by Wagner in unexpected ways. 'In order to represent the blazing flickering flames,' he observed, 'Wagner wrote a figure which is almost impossible for a first-rate soloist to play cleanly throughout. But when played by 16 to 32 violinists, the passage has such a marvellous, overwhelming effect that it is absolutely impossible to imagine a better representation of the blazing fire flickering in a thousand hues.' [3]

Rimsky-Korsakov, another master of instrumentation, remarked that 'Wagner's methods of orchestration struck Glazunov and me, and thenceforth his devices gradually came to form part of our orchestral tricks of the trade'. Bruckner, Mahler, Strauss, Debussy, Ravel, Scriabin, Dvorak, Schoenberg, Pfitzner, and many others down to our own day, have been inheritors of Wagner's innovations and, in turn, have influenced others.

His orchestra for the *Ring* was large compared with contemporary practice, and it is still large by modern standards. The original manuscript indicated a total of 107 instruments, which was increased to 119 for the premier performance in 1876. For the second production at Bayreuth in 1896, the number was increased to 124. Compare this with the Dresden orchestra, one of the finest and largest in Europe, which had only forty players in 1783, and even in the late 1840s just sixty-six players. The Leipzig Gewandhaus orchestra had thirty-five players in the 1840s. In 1838, when Wagner had been musical director in Riga, he conducted performances of six of Beethoven's symphonies with orchestras of just twenty-four musicians. Against such numbers, an orchestra of 119 players must have seemed a wanton extravagance – until people heard what it could do.[4]

In *Siegfried*, the orchestral sound is extraordinarily descriptive. Viewing the work as a whole, we can recognise a general movement of tone and texture from darkness to light, from the hidden dangers of Mime's cave and the depths of the forest to the clarity and transparency of Brünnhilde's mountain top. The first and third scenes of Act One have a dark and ominous mood, emphasised by the use of violas, lower strings, bassoons and tubas. Against this dark background, the two tenor voices of Siegfried and Mime are thrown into high relief. The presence of Fafner, who is never far from Mime's mind, is made palpable by the tubas. The violas in particular, come into their own in the early part of *Siegfried*, for they are able to express, as nothing else can, the dark and scheming nature of Mime. The Wanderer, on the other hand, radiates dignity and a kind of grandeur, not only because of what he sings and the form in which he sings it, but also because of the musical aura which surrounds him. The changes in feeling and mood are clearly apparent during the exchanges between Mime and the Wanderer as they ask each other questions.

Just when the audience is beginning to wonder if all of the action is over, Wagner gives us one of the most energetic scenes in the musical theatre. Siegfried returns to collect his sword, only to find Mime still cowering behind his anvil. In the conversation which follows, Mime tries to explain to Siegfried what fear is all about. He describes the apparition which he had seen in the dark forest, and the orchestra again conjures up the flashing, flickering lights and murmuring noises. But to Siegfried, fear is still incomprehensible, and this is reflected in the orchestra which repeats Mime's fevered imagery without the terror and anxiety. Mime then tells Siegfried about Fafner, and says that he will learn all about fear by confronting the dragon in its lair.

Siegfried is anxious to do just that, but since Mime is clearly unable to repair the sword *Notung*, Siegfried decides to do it himself. He piles charcoal on the hearth and fans the fire. He files the sword fragments into small pieces and puts them into a crucible which he then heats, using the bellows to raise the temperature of the flames. While Siegfried is engaged in smelting and toiling away at the bellows, Mime is equally busy mixing his poisonous brew. Their singing continues in deadly counterpoint.

The contents of the crucible are poured into a mould, which is then plunged into water with much hissing of steam. The orchestra works overtime to produce an amazing variety of sound effects. The mould is thrust back into the fire, then broken open, and the glowing steel is placed on the anvil. Siegfried sings his forging song as he strikes the blade with his hammer. Sparks fly and Mime savours the prospect of getting rid of this tiresome boy for ever.

When his work is finished, Siegfried hails the return of his father's sword and holds it aloft. He then brings it down violently on the anvil, which splits in half with a crash, causing Mime to fall to the ground with fright. The splitting of the anvil is not just a piece of theatricality. It has its origins both in a Norse saga of the thirteenth century, *Thidrekssaga*, in which Sigurd shatters Mimir's anvil with a hammer, and in the tale of the youth who did not know fear, in which the boy shatters an anvil with an axe.

In his autobiography, *Mein Leben*, Wagner describes how, as a nine-year-old boy living in Leipzig, he had met the composer Carl Maria von Weber, who visited the family home on a number of occasions. He was impressed, he said, by Weber's 'refined, delicate and spiritual appearance' and by his enquiries as to the young Richard's ambitions. But most of all, wrote Wagner, he was impressed by the music of Weber's most famous opera, *Der Freischütz*, which had had its premier the year before. Nothing, Wagner recalled, moved him more strongly than this music, even as a nine-year-old!

Der Freischütz was a milestone on the road to a recognisably German operatic genre and to the development of romantic opera in general. It is easy to find Weberian influences in Wagner's early works, but by the time of the *Ring*, these have all but disappeared, with one notable exception: in *Siegfried*. The spooky atmosphere of the wolf's glen in *Der Freischütz* finds a clear echo in the scene in the forest at night, during which firstly Alberich, then Wotan, and then Siegfried and Mime make their appearance at the entrance to Fafner's cave. In both cases, the tremolo strings and soft, ominous kettle drums create the unmistakable mood of the supernatural. It is Wagner's homage to his great predecessor. There is even, in D*er Freischütz*, an embryonic suggestion of the Forest Murmurs, which will feature a little later in Act Two of *Siegfried*.

The curtain rises on Alberich, keeping watch outside Fafner's cave. A bluish light in the forest heralds the appearance of the Wanderer. A tense conversation ensues, during which the Wanderer informs Alberich (and us) that a hero approaches who will free the golden hoard, that Mime is Alberich's rival for the gold, that Fafner will be killed and the ring pass to a new owner.

Eventually, the Wanderer awakens Fafner and warns him that he is in danger. He offers the dragon safety if he will give up the golden hoard, but Fafner declines the offer. Alberich then offers to take the ring off his hands whilst leaving the rest of the treasure intact. Again, Fafner declines and asks just to be left alone to sleep. He yawns. Yawning dragons? If anyone wonders about Wagner's sense of humour, Act Two of *Siegfried* provides plenty of examples.

The Wanderer laughs and departs, warning Alberich to beware of his brother, Mime. As day begins to dawn, Alberich hides himself in a rocky cleft on one side of the cave, and the stage remains empty for some moments. Then Mime and Siegfried arrive.

What should we make of this dragon who is so reluctant to stir from his cave? From one perspective, Fafner represents the pointlessness of hoarding wealth. The treasure in his cave is the equivalent of money under the bed, talent not developed, resources left unused. But a dragon also symbolises the fears which we all carry about within us – except Siegfried of course. Our own personal dragons are the things which we regard as frightening and intimidating, and which we must overcome if we are to grow as individuals.

Our irrational prejudices are dragons too. Siegfried has no quarrel with Fafner, but his mind has been moulded by Mime. He intends to destroy Fafner, just as Mime has told him to. Actually, the ring is perfectly harmless as long as Fafner has it, because he wishes only to guard it, not use it. If it is not to be returned to the Rhinemaidens, surely the next best thing is for it to remain in Fafner's possession. By killing the dragon and freeing the ring, Siegfried is only putting it back in the public domain where it can do more harm. Of course, it is not Siegfried of his own volition who wants to do this but Siegfried under the malign influence of

Mime. Unfortunately, this is not the last occasion on which Siegfried will be manipulated in this way.

Mime provides the obligatory warnings about the Dragon's jaws, its corrosive saliva and its deadly tail. Siegfried promises to watch out for all of these dangers and ascertains that the beast's heart is in the usual place. Mime then goes off to cool himself in a stream and leaves the boy to rest in the shade of a linden tree. Siegfried muses on what his father must have been like – like him perhaps – and then he tries to imagine his mother. The music takes on a most delicate and tender quality and, for the first time, we feel sympathy for Siegfried, who is revealed as being desperately lonely. He will do anything for true companionship.

We hear the gentle rustling of the Forest Murmurs, and nature is evoked with the most exquisite orchestral writing. Years later, Cosima Wagner recorded in her diary her husband's comments during a performance of the *Siegfried Idyll*, which draws on the music of Acts Two and Three of *Siegfried*. She wrote: 'What a sound such a wind instrument makes!' Richard says. 'The strings are like a forest, and the woodwinds like the birds within it.' [5]

In his desire to communicate with a woodbird which sings in the branches above him, Siegfried cuts a reed and fashions it into a simple pipe. His attempts to mimic the bird are woeful and, in the end, he gives up and just blows his horn instead. This wakens the dragon. In the fight which ensues, Fafner is mortally wounded but asks, before he dies, who the brave boy is who has finished him off. Siegfried cannot say who he is, other than that he is called Siegfried. Fafner, more giant than dragon at the moment of his death, tells him in a moving passage that the brothers Fasolt and Fafner are now both victims of the cursed gold, and he warns of Mime's murderous intentions. Then, repeating the young hero's name, he expires.

When Siegfried removes his sword from Fafner's heart, some

of the dragon's blood gets smeared on his fingers. Involuntarily, he puts his fingers to his mouth and, when he tastes the blood, he finds that he can understand what the Woodbird is saying: 'Hei! Siegfried has won now the Nibelung hoard! Now let him find it within Fafner's cave! The Tarnhelm that's his will assist him with marvellous deeds. If he could discover the ring it would make him lord of the world.' Thus, prompted by the woodbird, Siegfried enters the cave. As he disappears, the unholy Nibelung brothers, Alberich and Mime, emerge from the rocky cleft and the forest, respectively, and start bickering about which of them should have the ring and the other treasures.

Wagner handles the scene which follows with consummate skill. The rivalry of the brothers takes the form of a scherzo, whose tricky rhythms and insistent phrases reveal all too clearly the essential natures of Alberich and Mime. Each claims the gold for his own, and bids the other to keep his greedy eyes and hands off it. 'It is mine by right,' claims Alberich, 'for who robbed the Rhine of its gold and who wrought the spell of the ring?' 'And who,' counters Mime, 'made the Tarnhelm for you?' So the petulant dialogue goes on, each taunting and attacking the other.

At last, Alberich wears Mime down and the latter suggests a compromise: Alberich can keep the ring if Mime can have the Tarnhelm. Alberich rejects this with a scornful laugh: would he ever be safe in his sleep if Mime had the Tarnhelm, which gives invisibility to its wearer? Beside himself with rage, Mime shrieks, 'Not the Tarnhelm? Do I get nothing then?' Alberich declares that he will not give him even a nail, to which Mime responds that he will call for support from Siegfried, who will avenge him with his sword on his 'dear brother'. In this amazing scene, the vocal lines are written in 6/8 time, while the orchestral parts are in 2/4 time.

Siegfried reappears from the cave with only two items – the Tarnhelm and the ring. He does not really understand what they are and has only taken them because the bird counselled him to do so. They are tokens of his triumph over Fafner. He thrusts the Tarnhelm into his belt and puts the ring on his finger. Once more the bird speaks to him, warning him of Mime's treachery and telling him that, having tasted the blood of the dragon, he will be able to see through the dwarf's words to the secret intentions of his heart. Mime slinks back on stage and, with oily hypocrisy, greets the young dragon-slayer.

Siegfried says that he regrets Fafner's death, especially when more evil figures still roam free, and adds that he hates him who provoked the fight more than he hated the dragon. Mime then imagines himself saying flattering and deceiving things to Siegfried, but the latter can now understand what the dwarf really intends, which is to murder Siegfried and take all that he has won. Mime becomes increasingly perplexed because Siegfried seems to know what is really in his mind as opposed to what he thinks he is saying. The orchestra conveys simulated affection and concern, while Mime's words reveal exactly the opposite. Dramatically, this is a most daring device and it works superbly.

As Mime tries, in honeyed tones, to give Siegfried a poisoned draught, he is all the while revealing that when the boy is unconscious he will hack off his head. Provoked beyond endurance, Siegfried raises his sword and, with a single blow, strikes Mime dead. Alberich's mocking laughter rings out from the cleft nearby. Siegfried drags Mime's body on to the golden hoard which he had so long desired and which can now be his for ever.

Now Siegfried is truly alone in the world. Once again the Woodbird comes to his aid and tells him of a glorious bride: Brünnhilde, who awaits him on a rocky height surrounded by a fierce flickering fire. Excited at the prospect of finding a companion, Siegfried sets off after the bird which, at first, teases him by flying around in circles and then going hither and thither, before heading off towards Brünnhilde's rock. At last, Siegfried will discover fear, not in the depths of the forest nor in a dragon's cave, but in the arms of a woman.

In June 1857 Wagner abandoned work on *Siegfried* to start on *Tristan und Isolde*. There is plenty of evidence that the world of *Tristan* was occupying more and more of his thoughts while he was working on the *Ring* and that, at last, he could contain himself no longer and had to do something about it. There are scraps of music foreshadowing what was to come, and there are letters on the subject which are most revealing. For example, he wrote to the Princess Marie Wittgenstein in August 1857: 'The second act is finished. Fafner is dead, and Siegfried has run after the Woodbird, but while working on *Siegfried*, *Tristan* has given me no peace. In fact, I have been working simultaneously on both.' He did a little more work on *Siegfried* in July of that year and completed the orchestral draft of Act Two in August but, after that, work on the *Ring* was left in abeyance for a full twelve years, until 1869. Inevitably, when he did resume work, he was able to bring to Act Three of *Siegfried* and to all of the scoring of *Götterdämmerung* the wealth of experience gained in writing *Tristan* and *Meistersinger*, each in its own way a pinnacle of Western art.

From the opening bars of Act Three of *Siegfried* we can only marvel at the new facility with which Wagner handles his complex musical forces and elaborate thematic structures. Wotan is riding to see Erda to find out what the future holds. No fewer than nine motifs are woven into the prelude to Act Three to describe the god's search for answers, the turbulent state of his mind, and the drastic consequences of events which are now out of control.

We are a long way, conceptually, from Siegfried's forest; closer perhaps to the spirit of *Die Walküre*. The issues are of cosmic significance, and although Wotan is still in the guise of the

Wanderer, he is no longer the rather genial, if awe-inspiring figure who bantered with Mime in their game of Trivial Pursuit. He summons Erda from her sleep and pours out his troubled heart to her. He is desperate for her wisdom and advice. She tells him to consult her daughters, the Norns who spin the rope of world knowledge which binds past, present and future. This is not what the Wanderer wants to hear. Erda recalls that she once bore to Wotan a maiden, Brünnhilde, who is both brave and wise. Why doesn't he consult her? The Wanderer replies that Brünnhilde has been condemned to sleep and to mortality for her wilfulness. This astonishes Erda, for she knows that the very attributes that Wotan has condemned in their daughter characterise his own nature.

The world now seems upside down. Like Fafner, Erda just wants to return to her slumber. But the Wanderer won't let her go until she tells him how to deal with his worries. She replies unhelpfully that he is no longer what he purports to be and should not be disturbing her sleep. After a long silence, he brings himself to acknowledge the inevitability of change, the demise of the old moral order which he personifies, and the emergence of a new order to which the young Siegfried belongs. He bequeaths the future to the young Volsung who does not even know him but who is destined to awaken Brünnhilde. She, in turn, will set the world free.

This noble passage, in which the Wanderer accepts the inevitable, again demonstrates Wagner's ability to weave together many different motifs into a rich emotional fabric. Prominent amongst the motifs is a new and splendid one, usually referred to as the world's inheritance. I doubt if Wagner could have written this scene before he had written *Die Meistersinger*. There is more than a touch of Hans Sachs in the Wanderer in this last Act of *Siegfried*.

Erda descends once again into her timeless sleep, just as Siegfried appears in the distance. The Woodbird, which is leading him, takes one look at Wotan and flees in alarm. In the conversation that follows between the Wanderer and Siegfried, things go well enough for a while, but the Wanderer's probing questions begin to annoy Siegfried who comments rudely on the older man's appearance; he has lost one eye, and Siegfried threatens to put out his remaining one. The Wanderer bars the way with his spear and, in doing so, discloses that Siegfried's sword had been broken once before on this spear. The boy thinks that he has at last discovered his father's foe (which is not far from the truth) and, with a single blow, he slices the spear in half. Thus Siegmund is avenged. The Wanderer collects the broken pieces of the spear and tells Siegfried to proceed. He can stop him no longer.

In *Das Rheingold,* Wagner used some of his most descriptive writing in the transitional passages which link scenes: the movement from the River Rhine to the mountain top overlooking Valhalla, and the descent to and return from Nibelheim. Now he uses the same procedure to link the scene at the base of Brünnhilde's rock with that on the high place where she sleeps. However, what makes this extended musical interlude so interesting is that, as well as climbing upwards, Siegfried must pass through the sea of flames which surround the mountain.

The result is a dazzling picture in sound, drawing on a variety of motifs reviewing Siegfried's circumstances and state of mind while he presses on determinedly through the seething, flickering fire. The feeling of gradual ascent is conveyed by the movement of the orchestral texture from lower, darker, heavier sounds to higher, lighter, more transparent ones.

Finally, we leave the flames behind us and reach the brilliant sunlight and pure atmosphere of the mountain top where Brünnhilde sleeps. For the first time in several hours, we hear the orchestral sound of very high strings, woodwind chords, and the shimmering delicacy of the harp. The effect is magical.

The tenor playing Siegfried has been on stage for the best part of three hours before Brünnhilde is awakened. He is engaged in vigorous and demanding singing, has to act like a youngster less than half his age and undertake all kinds of energetic activity such as forging and fighting. The soprano playing Brünnhilde, on the other hand, has not sung a note in all this time and spends the first part of this final scene lying comfortably on some sort of bedding. One might assume therefore that, for Brünnhilde at least, this scene is a 'piece of cake'. Nothing could be further from the truth. Birgit Nilsson has commented that even if she sang as beautifully as ten angels, she could not compete with the incredibly vibrant 'awakening' music in the orchestra. Brünnhilde never seems to stop singing from the moment she is kissed until her last stratospheric high C.

Nellie Melba had a disastrous involvement with the *Siegfried* Brünnhilde, as she records in her autobiography.[6] She had long wanted to sing the role and had engaged a German language coach to train her. She secured a performance at the Metropolitan in 1896 (at the expense of her main artistic rival, Lillian Nordica, who was the resident Brünnhilde) but soon realised that she had made a great mistake. She said afterwards that she had felt as if she were struggling with something beyond her strength. She had had the sensation of suffocation, of battling with some immense monster – a very different feeling from the usual exaltation which she had experienced in other roles. When she returned to her dressing room, she sent for her manager and told him to tell the critics that she would never do that again, that it was beyond her and she had been a fool. For Melba, that was quite an admission.

When Siegfried reaches the summit of the mountain, he sees

Brünnhilde's horse, Grane, also asleep. In fairy-tales and legends of this type, animals behave very much like the humans to whom they are attached. So, for example, in the tale of *Briar-Rose*, when the princess pricks her finger and falls asleep, the household and all of the animals in the castle yard fall asleep at the same moment. They then awaken at the same moment too. In a sense, Grane is an extension or aspect of Brünnhilde's own personality.

Siegfried is attracted to the sleeping figure's shining armour and thinks, not unreasonably, that it covers another man. Remember, at this point he has never seen a woman. He removes the helmet and long curling hair tumbles out. He still thinks it is a man, albeit a rather fair one. Then he tries to undo the breastplate and, finding this difficult, uses his sword to cut through the rings of mail on each side. When the breastplate is removed, Brünnhilde lies before him in soft woman's drapery. He stares in amazement, his heart pounds and he is filled with a new emotion – fear. His first reaction is instinctively to call out to his mother. 'Mother! Mother!' he says, 'Remember me!' It is an unbearably touching moment. He tries to awaken the sleeping figure but she does not respond. Only when he presses his lips to hers does she stir. To music which seems to be quivering with life and pulsating with long-restrained energy, she slowly rises to a sitting position and greets the sun and the light.

Significantly, her first words are addressed not to the man before her but to the sun. However, these are, in a sense, one and the same. In Norse mythology, the cycles of nature were often symbolised poetically as the trials of love. Sigurd (Siegfried) could be interpreted as a sun lord who, armed with a sunbeam (the sword *Notung*) dispels the darkness. Brynhild (Brünnhilde) was the dawn-maiden whose path he crossed each morning. In greeting the sun, Brünnhilde is greeting Siegfried himself at the start of this day of days, ushered in with a kiss. As events unfold in

Götterdämmerung, the tragic separation and fiery reunion of the lovers mirrors the solar transit from dawn to dusk. Such was the symbolism of the old myths.

Brünnhilde's first words on her awakening, '*Heil dir, Sonne!*', which seem simple enough, have been variously translated as 'Hail to you, sun!' or ' Hail, Bright sunlight!' or 'Hail to thee, oh sun!' or 'Hail, my sunlight!' or 'I greet you, sun!', to quote just some versions. This points up the difficulties faced by any translator, especially if the intention is also to match the German metre or even approximate the sound of German syllables. The best modern English translation of *The Ring*, to my mind, is that by Andrew Porter, whose version is clear, sensible and singable, and carefully avoids unintentional humour. Porter advises against colloquialisms such as 'Hi there, sunshine!', for obvious reasons.

Brünnhilde rejoices when she learns that it is Siegfried who has made his way through the flames to claim her. Siegfried praises the mother who bore him and Brünnhilde echoes his words. She tells him that she had always loved him and had cared for and protected him even before he was born. Siegfried responds softly and shyly: 'So my mother did not die then?' In his innocence he hopes beyond hope that perhaps this is his mother returned to him, not from death but from sleep. Brünnhilde gently dissuades him: 'O innocent child, never more will you look on your mother. But we are one if you can grant me your love'.

Then there unfolds a rapturous love duet. At one point, Siegfried's ardour gets the better of him and Brünnhilde tears herself away and flees to the other side of the stage. She is finding it difficult to come to terms with her newly discovered humanity. Siegfried suggests that she is still sleeping, and he wants to awaken her to be his bride. Her mind is in turmoil, and now it is her turn to be afraid. She imagines that night has fallen and all kinds of horrors loom up in the dark. Siegfried sees only the beginnings of a new life; Brünnhilde predicts its end. Eventually, he succeeds in turning her mind to other things, and she responds with a tender assurance of her constancy and love.

The music which Wagner introduces at this point has been the subject of much comment and conjecture. It is well known to concert audiences from the opening bars of the *Siegfried Idyll*, written to celebrate Cosima's birthday on Christmas Day 1870 and the birth of their son Siegfried in the June of the previous year. The music, which appears to have even earlier origins, had a very personal significance for both Richard and Cosima and it is as if, for a moment, they had identified themselves completely with the heroic pair whose love for each other had been awakened on that sun-lit mountain top. Something of a musical gear change occurs when this passage begins, and commentators have had very mixed feelings about it. The main objection seems to be that it is an extended, self-contained melody bearing little relationship musically to what has gone before. It is also said that the words seem to have been forced to accommodate a predetermined melody, in contradiction of one of Wagner's main dramatic principles.

I would offer a few thoughts on this. It is true that Wagner considered it important to preserve the dramatic integrity of words and music; that is to say, both should be used in a complementary way to express the dramatic idea, and neither should be used simply as a peg on which to hang the other. However, we have also seen that he was quite willing to introduce extended lyrical passages when circumstances warranted this, especially to express feelings of love. He also breaks his own rule when other 'unusual' states of mind need to be expressed, and characters 'freeze the action', as it were, to enter a state of rhapsody or delirium or even just 'song'. In all of these cases, the extended melodic line is used to take characters out of themselves or at least out of the usual context of sung dialogue. Thus, we have Siegmund's Spring Song, Siegfried's Forging Song, Walter's Prize Song, the Quintet in *Meistersinger*, Wolfram's Song to the Evening Star in *Tannhäuser*, Tristan's delirium, Isolde's *Liebestod* and so on. It seems to me that Brünnhilde's soliloquy falls precisely into this category.

From this point until the end of the act, the lovers lose themselves in an ecstatic outpouring of joy. The language is rhapsodic and the lines are highly compressed. Robert Donington has described the mood as one of manic over-elatedness. It is certainly the antithesis of the sombre, sinister beginning to Act One. We have moved from scheming and ill will to the most blatant baring of souls and declarations of love. We have gone from the ominous depths of Mime's cave to the giddy heights of Brünnhilde's rock. In the rare atmosphere and dazzling sunlight, we share the feeling that nothing could possibly detract from this moment of happiness. The music swells into a torrent of joy which sweeps everything before it. 'Farewell, Walhall's glittering world,' sings Brünnhilde, 'Farewell splendour of the gods' ... 'Let the twilight of the gods – *Götterdämmerung* – now draw near' ... 'I live by the light of Siegfried's star ... radiant love and laughing death'.

Just as the rhapsodic love music of Siegmund and Sieglinde crowned the first Act of *Die Walküre*, so the ecstatic music of their son and the reborn Brünnhilde is the high point of *Siegfried*. In both cases, the outpouring of love and optimism seems rather exaggerated, but it prepares the way for a tragedy which, by contrast, will be all the more devastating.

Far behind us now is the innocent boy who tormented Mime with a forest bear, reforged *Notung*, slew the dragon and communed with nature. We are about to enter a very different world, a world of men and women, a savage and complex world conjured up by some of the most astounding music ever written.

For the moment, the lovers have thoughts only for one another, and we leave them in the euphoria of their mutual awakening to new life and love as the curtain falls on *Siegfried*, the second day of the Festival Play *Der Ring des Nibelungen*.

The Norse precursor of Siegfried roasts the heart of the dragon, Fafner. He is shown here sucking his thumb and accidentally tasting the dragon's blood, which enables him to understand the language of birds.
Twelfth-century woodcarving.

Götterdämmerung

Götterdämmerung, like Shakespeare's *King Lear* and the *Agamemnon* of Aeschylus, offers an uncompromising picture of human frailty. Such works shock and dismay, but they can also inspire hope for a better world. By the time we reach the closing bars of this, the last and greatest part of the *Ring*, we are meant to feel that a better and more humane world is not only desirable, but possible as well. Certainly, we will have experienced some of the most beautiful and passionate music ever written.

Götterdämmerung can be puzzling on first acquaintance, as it contains a number of paradoxes. Although its scale is prodigious, it is concerned not with the cosmic ambitions of gods and goddesses, giants and dwarfs, but the day-to-day relationships of men and women. Its action takes place in real time and space but its characters often have recourse to supernatural aids and remedies. Its principal figures, Siegfried and Brünnhilde, spend much of their time behaving in ways that are totally out of character. Finally, of all the dramas of the *Ring*, it seems to be the least faithful to Wagner's early theories of *Gesamtkunstwerk* (total work of art), since the music, especially the orchestral music, has a dominant role in advancing the drama.

It has been suggested that Wagner might have lost the plot

after so many years of working on his Nibelung story, that the work had become disjointed with its backwards expansion from one to four separate dramas, that his earliest *Ring* text and his most sophisticated musical score make uncomfortable bed-fellows, that he had abandoned his theories about new dramatic forms in favour of more traditional operatic practices, and that he just wanted to get the whole thing finished as quickly as possible and was careless about inconsistencies. I think we need to look a little deeper than this. After all, he had had more than twenty years to think about what he wanted to achieve.

Götterdämmerung is a work of mighty proportions, lasting four-and-a-half hours (not counting intervals), and the first act alone is longer than, say, the whole of *Tosca* or *La Bohème* or *Elektra*. It displays Wagner's genius for creating and sustaining moods, manipulating climaxes, and exploring the deeper recesses of the human psyche. However, some of its greatest innovations are to be found in musical details.

By the time Wagner was ready to begin composing the music of *Götterdämmerung* in 1870, two significant developments had occurred. Firstly, most of the *leitmotivs* that form the basic genetic material of the *Ring* – its DNA if you like – had already been determined in the earlier dramas. Secondly, he had acquired unbounded facility as a composer in the writing of *Das Rheingold*, *Die Walküre*, *Siegfried*, *Tristan und Isolde* and *Die Meistersinger von Nürnberg*. Consequently, he was now able to handle his musical material without detectable effort or self-consciousness.

Twenty years after he had first mapped out a new path in his treatise *Oper und Drama*, Wagner was supremely confident of both his materials and his abilities and had nothing more to prove. He was now able to give himself completely to his drama, and to treat its themes and their relationships with the utmost freedom – one might almost say abandon. He could pick up motifs and drop them again, snatch bits from this and elements from that, mix and blend with unstudied ease, and create a complete musical language with which to convey every nuance of the story, without being tied rigorously to the text. And all the while, this musical language poured forth – as the critic from *The Times* wrote after the first performance – like a wind that is always blowing or a stream that is always flowing. In short, Wagner had created his own dramatic universe, with its own laws and its own logic, and there was nothing he could not accomplish within it.

We enter this universe like travellers from another time and place, to observe the three Norns, the daughters of Erda, who spin the rope of world knowledge which binds past, present and future. It is night on the Valkyrie's rock and firelight shines from round about. There is, according to the stage directions, gloomy silence and stillness. The prelude is of the briefest kind, but such was Wagner's ability to conjure up mood and atmosphere that eighteen bars is all that is required to set the scene with great effect. The woodwind chords which had heralded Brünnhilde's awakening at the end of *Siegfried* had been in the bright keys of E minor and C major. *Götterdämmerung* opens with similar chords, but this time in the gloomy keys of E flat minor and C flat major. There could be no greater contrast with the euphoria of the closing scene of *Siegfried*, and yet it is achieved with the simplest of means. We know at once that all is not right with the world. The benign nature motif, first heard in *Rheingold*, is hybridised with the ring motif and produces, on muted strings, the strange, unworldly music of the Norns' rope of destiny.

One of the marvels of *Götterdämmerung* is the way in which, through harmonic design and instrumental colour, a sinister atmosphere pervades virtually all of the work. Many scenes are set in broad daylight but, somehow, the sun no longer shines as brightly as it did in the earlier works, and all nature seems burdened by things going wrong. Everywhere, the corrosive harmonies of the ring are eating their way into the score.

The Norns ponder with some anxiety the state of the world as they pass their golden rope from one to the other. Again, Wagner uses the rondo form in the musical structure. The Norns speak in poetic terms about the death of the world ash tree and the drying up of the spring of wisdom. They disclose that the remnants of the ash tree have been piled up around Valhalla to await the fire that will consume the gods. They tell of the greed that led to the theft of the Rhinegold and the making of the ring. The rope starts to fray. They speak of Alberich's curse. The rope breaks. Their wisdom ends. The Norns vanish. Day begins to dawn.

Softly, the horns give out the theme of Siegfried as hero, followed on the clarinet by that of Brünnhilde. The latter is carried higher and higher through the orchestra until it bursts gloriously onto the scene with the coming of day. Various themes are woven into the sound picture which follows, and the lovers emerge from their shelter. Brünnhilde is a Valkyrie no longer but, to use her words, she is strong in will and rich in love. Siegfried is about to set out on adventures and gives Brünnhilde the ring as a token of his love. He is, he says, not Siegfried but Brünnhilde's arm, endowed with her spirit. Her horse, Grane, will be his companion in the world of men which lies below. Amidst music of the greatest rapture, the pair farewell each other and Siegfried disappears from view. Then follows the extended orchestral interlude known as Siegfried's Journey to the Rhine.

This magnificent interlude is full of youthful vigour and energy, and motif after motif traces the young man's descent from the mountain and passage through the countryside until he reaches the broad expanse of the River Rhine. We are now well and truly in the world of human beings, rather than the timeless realm of mythology and fairy-tale.

Brünnhilde's horse, Grane, like his mistress, is no longer a supernatural being and walks on the ground instead of flying through the air. In most productions these days, Grane is conspicuous by his absence. Even the best-trained horses are not always reliable on stage. They can be distracting and are seldom satisfied with a supporting role. There is no place for them in modern, symbolic productions and even in old-fashioned, literal ones, they can look curiously out of place against painted scenery. But I see no reason why we shouldn't continue to talk about Grane even if we don't actually see him. After all, Brünnhilde and Siegfried talk about him, and even talk to him. Indeed, his greatest moment comes at the end of *Götterdämmerung* when Brünnhilde urges him to greet his master by carrying her into Siegfried's funeral pyre.

It is important to remember that *Der Ring des Nibelungen* is a 'Stage Festival Play for three days and a preliminary evening', to use Wagner's description. Note the words 'festival' and 'play'. It is a theatrical event to be presented according to the conventions of the musical theatre which are, inevitably, removed from everyday reality. They are concerned with representation rather than realism, with ideas rather than facts. The audience participates in the festival play through its own creative involvement; by using its understanding and imagination, even by being prepared to see horses where none are apparent!

Towards the end of Siegfried's Journey to the Rhine, the music, very gradually, begins to lose its vitality. The energy and confidence with which it began dissipate. When the curtain rises, we realise that a very different mood prevails in the palace which is before us: the hall of the Gibichungs on the banks of the Rhine. We are now at the true beginning of Act One of *Götterdämmerung*. All that has gone before has been by way of a prologue, reminding us of the mythological significance of what is about to unfold. Gunther and Gutrune, brother and sister, are the rulers of this place. With them lives their half-brother Hagen, son of Alberich.

Gunther is noble enough but he is somewhat weak of character. His sister is sweet and malleable. Hagen, on the other hand, is cold and sinister; a strong character but an evil one. The musical depiction of these characters is of the greatest importance in *Götterdämmerung*, and the motifs associated with them are strikingly apt. Gunther's music, for instance, suggests that he is outwardly bold but that his boldness is illusory. He will be a pawn in the hands of his half-brother. Gutrune's music is heart-rending. She is caught up in forces that are too much for her, and she too will fall victim to Hagen's evil ambition. There can be no doubt about Hagen's dark and sinister nature, which is laid out plainly in the music associated with him.

Gunther is very uncertain of himself and requires constant reassurance. He asks Hagen whether his fame along the Rhine is worthy of his father's name. Hagen replies that Gunther's fame is not what it should be because there are still things that he has not yet accomplished. Furthermore, he is still without a wife and Gutrune without a husband. Hagen suggests that Gunther's reputation would be enhanced if he won the hand of a particular woman whom he has in mind. She dwells on a rock surrounded by fire. But, adds Hagen, Gunther would not be able to penetrate the fire himself. That deed could only be accomplished by Siegfried the Volsung who, incidentally, would make a fine husband for Gutrune.

Hagen seems to be remarkably well informed, since he also knows that Siegfried has slain Fafner and won the hoard. Presumably he has learned all these things from his father, Alberich. Gunther reacts angrily, asking why Hagen should urge him to do the impossible. Hagen then sets out his plan. We hear the mysterious motif of the Tarnhelm in the orchestra as Hagen asks, 'What if Siegfried should bring home the bride to you, wouldn't Brünnhilde then be yours?' It is not clear at this point just what the Tarnhelm motif signifies, but this is a good example of the use of a motif of anticipation. In due course we learn that the Tarnhelm will indeed have an important part to play. Hagen then outlines a plan to administer a potion to Siegfried, so that he might forget all memories of Brünnhilde, go to her through the flames and bring her to Gunther.

As is the way of myth, no sooner does the conversation turn to Siegfried than the sound of his horn is heard in the distance. He has acquired a boat, and we imagine him rowing easily against the stream, with Grane the horse on board as well. Hagen hails him from the shore and he turns towards the bank. As he steps ashore, the trombones give out, with maximum force, the terrible motif of the curse. The tragedy of *Götterdämmerung* has begun.

Siegfried greets Gunther who makes him welcome and puts all that he has at his disposal. Siegfried responds that he has nothing to offer in return, other than himself and his sword. Rather pointedly, Hagen asks about the Nibelung's hoard, for Siegfried attaches so little importance to it that it had completely slipped his mind. He replies that most of it had been left in the dragon's cave, but he had taken the object which now hangs on his belt. He has no idea what it is. Hagen, who is certainly more worldly wise than Siegfried, explains that this is the Tarnhelm, which will disguise its wearer at will, or take him in the twinkling of an eye wherever he may wish to be. 'Did you take anything else,' asks Hagen? 'Only a ring,' Siegfried replies, 'and that is now worn by a fair woman.' Hagen knows at once that he means Brünnhilde.

Gutrune enters and the music reveals her gentle and all too trusting nature. She offers Siegfried a drinking-horn, welcoming him as a guest in Gibich's house. He drinks, and his thoughts turn to Brünnhilde. The music wells up with memories of his love for her. Then, an extraordinary thing happens. The potion of forgetfulness with which Gutrune had laced his drink, begins to take effect. It is an eerie and terrible moment, and the music describes it with wonderful expressiveness. The twisted harmonies reflect what is happening to Siegfried's brain. He struggles to remember, but to no avail.

The potion does its obliterating work, and now Siegfried cannot keep his eyes off Gutrune. He asks if Gunther has a wife. Gunther replies that he has his heart set on one who is beyond his reach; her home is on a towering rock, surrounded by fire. Only someone who can penetrate the fire would win Brünnhilde for wife. Siegfried repeats each of Gunther's sentences after him, as if dimly conscious that he should be remembering something important. However, in no time at all, the memories of those rapturous love duets on the Valkyrie's rock have gone completely. Even when Brünnhilde's name is mentioned, Siegfried betrays no glimmer of recognition.

As Hagen had anticipated, Siegfried offers to help Gunther by going through the fire to claim Brünnhilde for him. Using the Tarnhelm, he will change his form into that of Gunther. In return, Siegfried asks for the hand of Gutrune. Again and again, the motif of the curse surfaces in the orchestra, tainting the rest of the music and reminding us of its continuing destructive work. Gunther and Siegfried decide to pledge eternal loyalty to each other. Hagen fills a drinking-horn with fresh wine. He holds it out to the other two, each of whom cuts his arm with his sword and lets the blood fall into the wine. Then they swear blood-brotherhood before drinking from the horn in turn. The scene is chilling and barbaric.

Even more chilling is the atonement – if a brother breaks his bond, if a friend is false to a friend, then what has been drunk in drops today will flow in streams unceasing. Of course, neither believes that this will ever happen. Hagen cuts the horn in two so that it can never be used again, and explains that he had not joined in the oath because his blood runs pale and slow and cold. It would only poison their drink.

The two blood-brothers set off for the fiery rock. There, Gunther will hide while Siegfried assumes his appearance and abducts Brünnhilde. Hagen remains at the entrance to the Hall, to watch and wait. The sons of freedom, as he calls them, may despise him, but they will return with a bride for Gunther and the ring for Hagen. 'Then they shall serve the Nibelung's son.' Another orchestral interlude follows, during which Wagner demonstrates his remarkable ability to evoke character and mood with the most economical of means.

While Brünnhilde, on her mountain top, is lost in blissful memories of Siegfried, storm clouds gather, followed by the surprising arrival of one of her Valkyrie sisters, Waltraute, in a highly agitated state. Waltraute has come of her own accord to urge Brünnhilde to return the ring to the Rhinemaidens, so that the curse can be lifted from the gods and the world. In a long but moving monologue, Waltraute paints a sad picture of Wotan and the gods, sitting gloomily in Valhalla, awaiting their end. Brünnhilde is shocked at the suggestion that she should give up the ring. It means more to her than Valhalla or the gods, she says, for its golden gleam tells her 'Siegfried loves me! Siegfried loves me!' Her message for the gods is simple: she will never forsake love, and she will never part with the ring, even if Valhalla itself falls into ruins! So, Waltraute has her answer, and she rushes away in despair.

Evening has fallen and the glow from the fire that encircles the rock has become brighter. The flames leap and dance more wildly than usual and, suddenly, through the swirling but somehow more ominous music of the magic fire, the sound of a horn is heard with the motif of Siegfried, and then his horn call. Brünnhilde starts up in delight as she prepares to greet the returning hero.

Suddenly, Siegfried appears before her on a high rock, but he has the appearance of a stranger – Gunther. The horror of this moment cannot be described in words alone, and there are few more blood-curdling scenes in all opera. Brünnhilde cannot believe what she sees; a stranger has come through the flames.

When Wotan had first conceived her punishment, he had intended to leave her to the mercy of the first stranger who encountered her. Now, it seemed, this terrible fate had befallen her.

Recovering some of her composure, she asks who it is who dares to come to her. Siegfried, in a feigned and deeper voice, replies 'Brünnhild! A suitor has come. I have sought you through the flames. I claim you as my wife. Now you must follow me.' From the music that accompanies these words, we are left in no doubt that Hagen is the evil influence behind all that is happening.

In answer to her questions, Siegfried says that he is a Gibichung, and that his name is Gunther. Brünnhilde gives a despairing cry: 'Wotan! You vengeful and pitiless god! Now I know the true meaning of my sentence. I am condemned to shame and sorrow!' Siegfried (in the form of Gunther) tells her that there in the cave she must become his wife. Summoning her remaining strength, she holds out the ring towards him and invokes its power to protect her, but to no avail. It is Gunther's by a husband's right, says Siegfried, and promptly tears it from her finger. He then drives Brünnhilde before him into the cave. She is a shocked and broken woman. Siegfried draws his sword and, in his natural voice, cries, 'Now, *Notung*, witness here how I keep my vow. I keep my word to my brother. Separate me from Gunther's bride!' They disappear into the cave and the curtain falls.

In Act One of *Götterdämmerung*, we have seen some startling developments. As Erda had warned in *Rheingold*, Alberich has had a son, Hagen, by a mortal woman, just as Wotan had had a son, Siegmund, by a mortal woman. The marriage of gods or other mythical beings with men and women is common in both Greek and Norse mythology. The offspring of such marriages usually display distinctive personality traits, which can be very useful from a dramatic point of view. We do not know a lot about

Hagen at this stage, other than his determination to manipulate everyone in order to get hold of the ring. He is resentful, humourless and single-minded.

We have also seen the use of the potion of forgetfulness, a mind-bending drug which selectively blots out Siegfried's memories of Brünnhilde and makes him lust after Gutrune. What do we make of this? A modern audience might feel that recourse to such a device is an easy way out for the story-teller. After all, such potions are the stuff of fantasy. In the present context, we need to ask ourselves whether the story of Siegfried's memory loss and infatuation with Gutrune might not be just a case of a wandering eye in a virile young man a long way from home? Perhaps Siegfried's ardour cools as quickly as it overheats.

This view might be convincing were it not for his obvious feelings for Brünnhilde when his memory returns in the last scene, and his comment in the Rhinemaidens' scene in Act Three that he would happily have made the closer acquaintance of one of those watery nymphs had he not been betrothed to Gutrune! He is all alone when he says this and yet he thinks only of his betrothal to Gutrune, not his marriage to Brünnhilde. No, I am bound to conclude that Siegfried's underlying intentions are honourable and that the potion of forgetfulness, if not to be taken literally, might be regarded as a metaphor for Hagen's evil ability to cause naive, susceptible people to behave in completely uncharacteristic ways. (There are many Hagens in the world who seem to be able to do just that.) There is one other possible interpretation of Siegfried's fascination with Gutrune, but I shall come to that in a moment.

Finally, there is the assumption of Gunther's physical appearance by Siegfried in order to abduct Brünnhilde from the protective circle of fire. Shape-changing is another common feature of mythological stories and is certainly not just a Wagnerian device for livening up the drama. Wagner would have been familiar with many of the Greek poems and legends which refer to metamorphosis. The Greek gods changed their shape at the drop of a hat, assuming the form of animals, or masquerading as humans. For example, in the *Iliad*, Athene took the form of Hector's brother in order to lure the Trojan hero to his death at the hands of Achilles. Heroes and others could be transformed into plants or animals, and some shape-changers underwent a whole series of transformations of a magical kind.

But there is also a less mystical origin to the story of Siegfried's transformation into Gunther. In the thirteenth-century *Thidrekssaga* (Dietrich's saga), we learn that Brynhild had agreed to wed Gunther but refused to consummate the marriage. So, Sigfrid dressed himself in Gunther's clothes and raped her. Obviously, such an account was not appropriate in the particular context of Wagner's story (or having regard to nineteenth-century sensibilities) but echoes of it remain in the atmosphere of horror and violence preserved in the music.

There is something Shakespearian about the opening scene of Act Two of *Götterdämmerung*. I think it is one of the most fascinating scenes in the entire *Ring*. It is especially interesting in terms of characterisation: Wagner lets us see Alberich and Hagen, father and son, not as they appear to us but as they appear to themselves. Alberich is completely justified, in his own eyes, in wanting the ring, especially after the wrong done to him by Wotan. Hagen will be his agent.

Hagen is discovered, as we left him, on watch outside the hall of the Gibichungs. When the curtain rises, it is night. Now and then, the moonlight breaks through the clouds and the music mirrors this when the dark, syncopated orchestral sound is suddenly broken by very high entries on flutes and oboes. We see the hall from a slightly different angle, and Hagen sits sleeping, leaning against one of the doorposts. He is waiting for the return of Siegfried and Gunther.

Oddly enough, in *Götterdämmerung* the gods have no direct part to play. In this drama, they are acknowledged only by altar stones on the hillside – stones dedicated to Fricka, to Wotan, to Donner and the rest. It is as if they are just memories of a distant past.

When the clouds separate for a moment, we notice that Alberich is crouching motionless in front of Hagen. 'Are you sleeping Hagen, my son?' he asks. Hagen remains motionless as he answers, and the conversation which follows has a strange dream-like quality. But whose dream? Alberich urges his son to take the ring from Siegfried, for if it is returned to the Rhinemaidens, the gold and the power which it confers will be lost to the Nibelungs for ever. 'Be true, Hagen, my son! Trusty hero! Be true! Be true!' Alberich vanishes as day begins to dawn.

The dawning takes place first of all in the orchestra, by the almost imperceptible transition to new harmonies and new motifs. The latter are introduced so subtly that it is difficult to be sure just when the transition begins; the process is almost organic. Wagner was especially proud of his skill in this respect and once characterised composition as the art of transition. The first soft rays of morning are accompanied by a beautiful canon for the horns and by the gradual emergence of the theme associated with Hagen's sardonic nature, later used by the vassals in their coarse celebrations. Clearly, it is Hagen's day that is now dawning.

Siegfried appears suddenly beside the river, in the act of removing the Tarnhelm from his head – he has used its magic to transport himself in advance of Gunther and Brünnhilde. Hagen calls Gutrune from the hall and there is an exchange between her and Siegfried, during which Siegfried reports on what had happened on the fiery rock. He has kept his part of the bargain; now he claims Gutrune as his own. The boat bringing Gunther and Brünnhilde is sighted and Hagen summons the Gibichung vassals to join the double wedding celebrations. He does this with a joke;

a typically rough Hagen joke to be sure, but we are, for a moment, shown another side of his character which becomes all the more convincing because of it. He doesn't call the vassals to a wedding, but to war! 'Weapons! Weapons!' he calls, 'Bring your weapons! ... Enemies are here!' He blows a steerhorn and other steerhorns answer from different directions off stage. The vassals rush on singly and then in growing numbers, assembling on the shore in front of the hall. They burst into raucous laughter when they discover the real reason for their summons.

Then follows the only chorus in the *Ring*; but what a chorus it is! After several hours of high drama, the effect of this lusty, barbaric, slightly old-fashioned music is to release emotional tension and to refresh the listener. At the same time it provides an unforgettable aural image of the brutal world of these Rhine dwellers, the subjects of Gunther and Gutrune and their half-brother, Hagen. It also prepares us for one of the greatest scenes in the whole work, the quarrel between Brünnhilde and Siegfried.

When the excitement has died down, both couples arrive in front of the hall. In the course of his welcoming remarks, Gunther speaks the name Siegfried. Brünnhilde, who has kept her eyes lowered all this time, is startled to hear the name and looks up to see Siegfried standing in front of her. She stares at him in amazement. Siegfried calmly presents Gutrune to her, clearly oblivious to their earlier relationship and pretending not to know of more recent events. Her bewilderment is compounded when she sees the ring, now on Siegfried's finger. If anyone should be wearing the ring, she says, it is Gunther, since he had torn it from her hand. Gunther has no idea what she is talking about.

Hagen is beginning to relish the complications which are now developing, especially when Brünnhilde finally realises that it must have been Siegfried who stole the ring from her. Siegfried replies that no woman gave him the ring; he won it from the dragon Fafner. Either he is protecting Gunther, or he has been caught out and is too ashamed to own up. Hagen decides to capitalise on the situation by asking Brünnhilde if she can identify the ring. If indeed it is Gunther's, then Siegfried must have been unfaithful to his friend and should pay for his treachery. Thus we reach a critical point in the drama.

Brünnhilde concludes bitterly that she has been betrayed and announces that not Gunther but Siegfried is her husband and that they had consummated their love. Not surprisingly, this causes much consternation in the Gibichung camp. Siegfried, who remembers only their second meeting, when he was disguised as Gunther, denies that anything happened between them. His sword *Notung* had lain between them, he says, and he had been faithful to his oath of blood-brotherhood. A furious Brünnhilde responds that when Siegfried had been with her, *Notung* had hung on the wall of their cave. Now Gunther feels betrayed and challenges Siegfried to deny the accusation. Siegfried replies that he will swear his innocence on the point of a spear, and asks who will offer him one for the purpose? Hagen is quick to oblige.

Siegfried lays two fingers of his right hand upon the spear point and addresses it as 'Shining steel! Holiest weapon!' He swears that if he betrayed Gunther, this spear should strike him down. We know that eventually it will but, for the moment, he firmly believes in the truth of what he says and fears no consequences. Then it is Brünnhilde's turn. She seizes the spear point and dedicates it to Siegfried's death. To her mind, he has betrayed every vow.

Baffled by these developments, Siegfried can only conclude that the Tarnhelm had not worked its magic well enough and that his disguise on Brünnhilde's rock had not been successful. He says so to Gunther and then leads Gutrune and the others into the hall to commence the celebrations. Only Brünnhilde,

Gunther and Hagen remain behind.

It is difficult to imagine how Wagner could improve on what we have just heard, but he does just that with the trio which follows. This ensemble – one of the few in the *Ring* – is often cited, together with the vassals' chorus, as evidence of a regression in Wagner's style; a return to more traditional operatic forms. There may be some truth in this, resulting perhaps from a text which predates the music by some twenty-four years.

However, I am more inclined to the view that the trio and the chorus (and other instances of 'regression' which people have identified in *Götterdämmerung*) are simply musical forms deliberately chosen because they best serve Wagner's dramatic purposes. When he came to write the music in 1872, he could quite easily have recast these 1848 words if he had wanted to. That he did not do so, suggests that he had another purpose in mind. In any event, it is just as well that the trio survived because it is, dramatically, one of the greatest moments in the *Ring*.

Brünnhilde calls for vengeance, and Hagen decides how he will kill Siegfried. He will plunge his spear into Siegfried's back because, according to Brünnhilde, only his back remained unprotected by her charms. Siegfried would never turn away from an enemy. In non-magical terms, we can interpret this to mean that because Siegfried is exceptionally courageous, no enemy could hope to get the better of him in honourable combat. Only a cowardly attack from behind could succeed.

The third conspirator, Gunther, is misery personified and is taunted by Brünnhilde for being a pitiful creature who cannot even do his own dirty work. Hagen tells him that he should expect 'no help from brain, no help from hand'. His only hope is 'Siegfried's death!' Gunther recoils at this idea and the orchestra refers pointedly to the motif of blood-brotherhood. Hagen persuades him that Siegfried has betrayed his oath and now can atone only with his blood. Brünnhilde replies that all the blood in the world could not wash away the guilt of those who have betrayed her but, she agrees, Siegfried must die. Hagen reminds Gunther that Siegfried's death will bring him the Nibelung's ring. Gunther is worried about the effect on his sister, the gentle Gutrune, but at last, he too agrees, Siegfried must die. Hagen decides that, in order to protect his half-sister's sensibilities, Siegfried's death will be staged to resemble a hunting accident involving a wild boar. And so this great and terrible trio reaches a climax with unanimity on Siegfried's untimely end.

Another composer might have brought down the curtain at this point, but Wagner has one more dramatic card to play. The touching music of Gutrune comes to our ears and a joyful bridal procession emerges from the hall. Siegfried and Gutrune are carried shoulder high; Siegfried on a shield. We know that he will soon return again to the hall on a shield, not for a wedding, but in death. The path is strewn with flowers, and sacrificial beasts are led to the altars of the gods. Gutrune smiles at Brünnhilde and signals her to join the festivities, but receives no response. The music of merry-making is intermingled with the sinister motifs of Hagen and of vengeance. Reluctantly, the conspirators join the procession, and the curtain falls on an act which must surely rank as Wagner's supreme achievement in the field of music drama.

Act Two has taken the drama in new and dangerous directions. Alberich has returned to offer his own ambition and resentment as added incentives for Hagen's actions. Hagen, we know, is jealous of his half-brother and -sister, whose legitimacy he envies. He has his own reasons for getting hold of the ring. Indeed, there is some evidence that Hagen is not very susceptible to his father's entreaties, though their objectives coincide. Alberich keeps addressing him as 'Hagen, my son', but the most affectionate name that Hagen can give his father is 'crafty dwarf'. He also reminds Alberich vindictively that it was with gold that he had bought his mother. But before we become too sympathetic towards Alberich, we should heed his own admission that he had always encouraged in Hagen a deadly hatred of Siegfried. Vengeance is what he desires, and vengeance is what Hagen, in the end, will give him.

We saw the worst side of the new Siegfried at the end of Act One. Now we witness a similar development in the character of Brünnhilde. She has every reason to be angry and resentful. She has learnt the truth of Siegfried's masquerade as Gunther and is smarting at his treatment of her. Furthermore, Siegfried's answers about their time together were obviously at odds with her own recollections. But does any of this warrant his murder? She has become so outraged – one might even say deranged – that she is willing to be Hagen's accomplice, dedicating the spear to Siegfried's death, disclosing his area of vulnerability and inciting Hagen to avenge her. By these actions, Brünnhilde is just as guilty as Hagen of Siegfried's murder. It seems hard to credit that this is the same Brünnhilde who, in the presence of Sieglinde, had gloried in the thought of Siegfried's birth, had been a noble Valkyrie and daughter, and had then been a loving woman and wife.

And what of the unfortunate brother and sister, Gunther and Gutrune? They are victims of forces beyond their understanding, just like that other brother and sister, Siegmund and Sieglinde. There are some interesting parallels between the Volsung and the Gibichung siblings. Of course, Gutrune's lover is not her brother. But he is her brother's blood-brother, which makes him, if you like, her brother once removed. From Sieglinde, Siegmund received the water of life as he lay exhausted in the house of his enemy, and it was over a drinking-horn of mead that their love for one another was kindled. From Gutrune, Siegfried received the potion of forgetfulness in the hall of his enemy, and it was over that drinking-horn that their love for one another was kindled. Hagen stands in the same dramatic relationship to Gutrune as did Hunding to Sieglinde, and each killed their respective enemy with a spear – Siegmund receiving it in the chest and his son Siegfried in the back. In both cases, Brünnhilde was involved, but in contrary ways. She had tried, compassionately, to save Siegmund and in doing so had earned the wrath of Wotan and the gratitude of Sieglinde. She, misguidedly, encourages the murder of Siegfried and in doing so earns the gratitude of Wotan's dark counterpart, Alberich, and the curses of Gutrune.

It is the gentle, vulnerable, appealing Gutrune, not the wild and formidable Brünnhilde, who is most like the mother Siegfried longed for. The characters of Sieglinde and Gutrune must have had similarities in Wagner's mind, for he considered using the same soprano, Mathilde Weckerlin, for both roles in the first production. In the end, she sang only Gutrune. Could it be that Siegfried was drawn, subconsciously, to Gutrune because, in her, he sensed similarities with his mother?

In mythology, magic (such as the potion of forgetfulness) symbolises any work of the unconscious which is not understood. Siegfried would hardly have understood the forces which compelled him, even after his encounter with Brünnhilde, to yearn still for his mother. Such feelings towards a mother are not usually confused with feelings towards a wife, although they may be, as in the so-called Oedipus complex, an infantile fixation on the mother. Siegfried's rather peculiar upbringing may have made him vulnerable to such a disorder. Of significance, too, for anyone familiar with the Oedipus story, is the fact that Siegfried had killed Mime, who had been *in loco parentis* for his father, and who had kept the identity of Siegfried's mother to himself for many years.

Could it be that Brünnhilde senses something deeper than ordinary attraction in Siegfried's feelings for Gutrune? After all,

Brünnhilde is the only one present who had actually known his mother and she understands Siegfried's susceptibilities in this regard.

In Act Three of *Götterdämmerung*, an important change in mood and atmosphere takes place. Acts One and Two had involved strong characterisations, highly charged relationships and violent emotions. The characters of Siegfried and Brünnhilde underwent some very peculiar developments, each being distorted almost beyond recognition under the malign influence of Hagen. Now they recover their true natures and rise above the evil which had so corrupted their view of one another. In musical terms, Wagner accomplishes this by recapturing some of the lyrical atmosphere of the earlier dramas. Lyricism, as I have already suggested, was inseparable from love in Wagner's thinking. A complete reversion is not possible; too much has occurred that cannot be undone. However, enough of the earlier world of innocence is recreated to remind us of what has been lost, and to make the tragic events which are to come seem almost unbearably poignant.

The earliest expression of lyricism in *The Ring* centres on the Rhinemaidens in *Das Rheingold*. Now, in Act Three of *Götterdämmerung*, we hear them again, those naive creatures of the deep, lamenting the loss of their gold as they swim in the sparkling waters. This time however, the joy has gone from their song, and despite the great beauty and intricate filigree of the score, they are manifestly burdened with cares. A little later, when Siegfried begins to regain his memory and recounts how he listened to the Woodbird outside Fafner's cave, all of the beauties of nature come flooding back. Later still, when Brünnhilde realises that Siegfried 'the truest of all men, betrayed me, that I in grief may grow wise!' she acquires a nobility of character which transcends even that displayed in *Die Walküre*. Finally, the entire *Ring* is brought to a close with that most lyrical of outpourings, commonly called the motif of redemption through love, last associated with the frantic and exhausted Sieglinde responding to the news that she would bear the noblest of heroes. This ecstatic motif, with its promise of new life, is Wagner's ultimate affirmation that hope and love will endure when all else has gone; an optimistic notion that has nothing at all to do with the philosophy of Schopenhauer which coloured his thinking in the mid-1850s.

Before the curtain rises on the final Act of the *Ring*, hunting horns alert us to what is happening on stage. Then we see the valley through which the great river flows. The Rhinemaidens are waiting for Siegfried, who is hunting with Gunther and Hagen and their men. Siegfried becomes separated from the others and appears on the cliff overlooking the river. The Rhinemaidens tease him and demand the ring which gleams on his finger. He refuses to give it to them and says that his wife would scold him if he gave away his goods so easily. Perhaps she beats him, one of the Rhinemaidens suggests and, laughing, they dive under the water.

When they surface again, it is to tell him solemnly to keep the ring and guard it well until he discovers what ill fortune it brings. Their warning could not be plainer. Anyone who possesses it is doomed to death. As Siegfried slew the dragon so he himself shall be slain this very day unless he returns the ring to the river. He replies that as he was not deceived by their wiles, so he will not be moved by their threats. They persist with their warnings but Siegfried tells them that he despises the worldly power which the ring is said to bring. He would barter it for the grace of love, but never under a threat. He counts life and limb of no more worth than the clod of earth which he then picks up and throws over his shoulder. The Rhinemaidens decide to leave this madman and foretell that, this day, a woman shall inherit the ring; one who will do what they ask. When they have gone, Siegfried muses that, were it not for his betrothal to Gutrune, he would have taken advantage of one of these playful creatures. Clearly, he has not been listening to a word that they have said.

The other members of the hunting party arrive to rest and refresh themselves. During the exchanges which follow, Siegfried tells of his boyhood and of the remarkable things that had happened to him. The wonderful nature music of the previous drama floods into the orchestra, and Siegfried sings of the Woodbird which warned him about Mime and told him of the ring and the Tarnhelm. He repeats the bird's words and even the notes that it sang. Hagen drops the juice of a herb into Siegfried's drinking-horn and, gradually, his memory begins to return. The bird, he recalls, showed him where Brünnhilde lay, surrounded by fire. It is a moment of the greatest tenderness and, in a twinkling, we see the young Siegfried, the naive and innocent boy, restored to us again.

He had loosened her helm, he continues, his kiss had awakened her to life and, with a feeling like burning fire, she had held him in her arms. 'Like burning fire' – we know what that means, and so does Gunther who springs up in horror. It seems that Siegfried had betrayed him after all. Two ravens fly up from a bush; they are Wotan's ravens, flying to tell their master that the end is near. Siegfried turns to look at them and Hagen asks 'Can you understand the language of those ravens? Vengeance, they cry to me!' and with that he plunges his spear into Siegfried's back.

Siegfried swings around in an effort to crush Hagen with his shield but his strength fails him and he crashes to the ground. Hagen slips away into the shadows but the others, including a remorseful Gunther, surround and comfort the dying man. Then, in a truly inspirational touch, Wagner draws from the orchestra the high, pure sounds to which Brünnhilde first opened her eyes and greeted the sunlight. Siegfried asks who has put her back to sleep. He had awakened her once; now he awakens her again to the truth. He shall live in Brünnhilde's love. With her name on his lips, he sinks back and dies.

Night has fallen. At a signal from Gunther, the vassals raise Siegfried's body and carry it in solemn procession over the rocky heights. All the while, the orchestra pours forth the Funeral Music, the effect of which is overwhelming. Laid before us, one by one in their grandest forms, are the various motifs associated with Siegfried's life, punctuated repeatedly with the shock of his death. Mists rise from the Rhine, obscuring the scene, and when they disperse, we find ourselves again before the hall of the Gibichungs.

Gutrune leaves her bedchamber and comes into the hall. Evil dreams have kept her awake. She fancies that she has heard the sound of Siegfried's horn and the neigh of his horse. She has heard Brünnhilde's laughter and has seen her steal silently towards the Rhine. Hagen's voice comes out of the darkness, calling for torches and rousing everyone from their sleep. With deliberate heartlessness, he bids Gutrune greet Siegfried; the mighty hero has come home again.

Then Siegfried's body is set before her, to everyone's horror. Hagen explains unconvincingly that Siegfried has been killed by a boar. The shocked Gutrune accuses Gunther of murder and he in turn blames Hagen who, at last, admits to the deed and glories in it. When Hagen tries to claim the ring, Gunther insists that it is Gutrune's dowry and tries to stop him. They struggle and Gunther is struck dead. Hagen goes to remove the ring from Siegfried's finger but, eerily, the hero's hand rises threateningly by itself.

Then Brünnhilde steps forward. From the Rhinemaidens she has learned how she and Siegfried have been the unwitting victims of Wotan's desperate bid to hold onto power. She instructs the vassals to erect a funeral pyre and to lift Siegfried's body on to it. Completely in command of events, Brünnhilde takes the ring and declares that it will be returned to the Rhinemaidens after being cleansed by fire. Then she takes a fiery brand and lifts it high. 'Fly home, you ravens!' she cries; 'tell Wotan what you have learned here by the Rhine! Wend your way to Brünnhilde's rock and bid Loge hasten to Valhalla, for the end of the gods comes at last! So I cast this brand on Valhalla's glittering towers!' Brünnhilde throws the brand on to the pyre which breaks into flame. Her horse is brought to her and she speaks loving words to it about joining their hero in a fiery death. Then they leap into the flames.

According to Wagner's stage directions, the pyre blazes up, catching hold of the hall, the river swells mightily and pours its flood over the fire. The three Rhinemaidens swim forward to recover the ring. Hagen plunges into the river, still intent on claiming the ring, Alberich's ring. The Rhinemaidens draw him below the waves in an embrace denied his father before he had renounced love and set the whole drama in motion. The hall crashes in ruins and, in the fiery glow in the distance, Valhalla is seen, with the gods and heroes assembled. The men and women who have gathered near the river, look on fearfully. Fire seizes upon the hall of the gods, and when this is entirely hidden by flames, the curtain falls.

All this time, the orchestra has been weaving together numerous references to the events that have led to this tremendous conclusion. We hear again of the power of the gods and their downfall, Siegfried of glorious memory, and the Rhinemaidens joyously reunited with their gold. Then comes the sonorous motif associated with the majesty of Valhalla, before it is consumed in the flickering music of the magic fire. At last, only the high, sweet strains of the motif of redemption through love remain to point the way to a new beginning.

The detailed stage directions that accompany the final pages of the score are seldom taken literally these days and, frankly, there is no need for them to be. Wagner, for all his individuality, was a practical man of the theatre and he knew what the theatre did best. His priority was not outward display but inner meaning. The staging, just as much as music and words, had to serve this inner meaning. This was something he had felt strongly about since the days when, after his first successful opera, *Rienzi*, he had turned his back on the grand operatic style of Meyerbeer, with its emphasis on spectacle and theatricality and use of Italian and French conventions.

The textual ending of *Götterdämmerung* was the subject of at least nine revisions by Wagner, as he tried to make up his mind about the implications of the whole work. In early drafts, the ring was to be restored to the Rhine, Alberich and the Nibelungs were to be free again, the gods were to be forgiven for their wrongdoing, and Brünnhilde was to proclaim Wotan's power for all eternity. Wagner wrote several versions of this.

An important influence on his thinking at that time appears to have been the philosopher Ludwig Feuerbach, to whom he dedicated his 1849 monograph, *The Art-Work of the Future*. Feuerbach's humanist view prompted a final scene which elevated love above material possessions, authority, convention and even fate, to which the gods were subject as much as anyone else.

Then Wagner decided that the gods should be destroyed by fire. A marginal note about this in his own hand in 1851 reads 'self-annihilation of the gods'. He then discovered Schopenhauer, and his focus changed to the annihilation of the will and complete self-abnegation as offering the only true means of redemption: the bliss of extinction.

So, in 1856, the ending was changed yet again and included various Buddhist references. In this version, Brünnhilde's peroration over Siegfried's funeral pyre contained the following words: 'I flee for ever from the home of delusion; the open gates to eternal becoming I close behind me. To the holiest chosen land, free from desire and delusion the goal of world-wandering, redeemed from rebirth, the enlightened one now goes'. It is fascinating to contemplate the idea of Brünnhilde as a Buddha, but that is precisely what Wagner had in mind in 1856.

In fact, in that year he had also drafted a prose sketch for a drama with an entirely Buddhist theme, called *Die Sieger* (*The Victors*), but did not proceed with it; just as, eight years earlier, he had abandoned the draft of *Jesus von Nazareth* (*Jesus of Nazareth*). Only later, in *Parsifal*, did he attempt to combine both Christian and Buddhist ideas in a unique and controversial view of the human spirit.

When he came to write the music for Act Three of *Götterdämmerung* in 1872, his solution was to combine the inevitable destruction of the old order with a belief in the regenerative power of love.

Wagner once referred to *Götterdämmerung* as 'a tragedy of fate'. The gods, giants, dwarfs and humans are all trapped in a fateful web, from which they struggle, in their own ways, to be free. In the end, it is only by the destruction of the existing order in its entirety, and through the agency of love, that the human race can make a new beginning. Brünnhilde has the wisdom to see this at the end and, by her own sacrifice, sets in motion events which, ultimately, make possible a better world.

The German word *Dämmerung* means not only 'twilight' in the sense of 'dusk', but also 'dawn'. So, even the title of the drama carries the connotation of a beginning as well as an end, which is difficult to convey in a single English word. The death of Siegfried and the destruction of the gods are cataclysmic events but, in the language of myth, death symbolises transformation. Seen in its entirety then, the musical spirit of Act Three of *Götterdämmerung* is essentially lyrical, love-asserting and life-affirming.

I said at the outset that the *Ring* is a drama of ideas and that, ultimately, it is about us all. It is a parable of human folly and frailty, which uses mythology and music to tell its story. Its philosophical roots belong to the Europe of the industrial revolution, a time of unparalleled social and political change. But, like all great works of art, it really belongs to no particular time or circumstances and it is capable of, indeed demands, constant reinterpretation.

During the many years which passed between the first sketch for the *Ring* in 1848 and its completion in 1874, Wagner ventured on numerous occasions to comment on his intentions and to explain the meaning which lay behind aspects of the narrative. However, because he did not, himself, maintain a consistent view on every point over this long period of time, it is impossible to say that *The Ring* signifies this and only this, or that and only that. He came to realise that he was in danger of contradicting himself by being too specific in his interpretations, and said as much in a letter to his friend Röckel as early as 1856:

> How can an artist expect that what he felt intuitively should be perfectly realised by others, seeing that he himself feels in the presence of the work, if it is true Art, that he is confronted by a riddle about which he too might have illusions just as another might.

However, one thing that did remain remarkably constant was the integrity of Wagner's musical language, from the opening E flat on the double basses in *Rheingold* to the closing D-flat chord in *Götterdämmerung*. We can only marvel at the infinitely flexible system of motifs which thread their way through the four dramas, his masterly handling of orchestral colour and texture, the expressiveness of his harmonies which convey, immediately and economically, the essence of a character or mood, and, above all, the skill with which he used all of these things as the raw material for a whole new mode of dramatic expression.

The critic Wilhelm Mohr, who attended the first performance, wrote afterwards that Wagner had 'won the battle' in the one area in which he was not trying to win it, namely in the field of music. The victory had gone to Wagner the musician, he said,

> because of his principles, irrespective of his principles, and contrary to his principles, he has created beauty, life in its fullness, and has brought into being musico-dramatic creations of a totally new kind. The old form has not been destroyed in this new beauty but has undergone a transformation like that of Siegfried's sword, *Notung*, which was filed down, melted, recast and forged ...

It is a moot point whether Wagner's philosophical notions came first and were then given form by the music, or he looked for ideas which seemed promising vehicles for the music which welled up naturally within him. Many people would be inclined to think the former, but I think that the latter is closer to the mark. The best guide to his practices in this regard is to be found in a letter of 1856 to August Röckel, in which he said:

> While, as an artist, I *felt* with such convincing certainty that all my creations took their colouring from my feelings, as a philosopher I sought to discover a totally opposite interpretation of the world. This interpretation once discovered, I obstinately held to it, though, to my own surprise, I found that invariably it had to be abandoned when confronted by my spontaneous and purely objective artistic intuitions.

Whatever one might think of Wagner's idiosyncratic philosophical ideas, it is in the music that his true genius lay, and he came to trust his artistic judgement far more than the polemic that so distracted and even misled readers of his own and later times.

The music of Richard Wagner is no longer new, and *The Ring* has been performed on countless occasions over the past century-and-a-quarter. Nevertheless, it continues to be staged somewhere in the world each year, and performances are invariably sold out. No fewer than twelve separate productions of *The Ring*, or its constituent parts, are listed to be performed in Europe, America and Australia between November 1998 and June 1999. Audio and video recordings of *The Ring* have never been more plentiful or accessible.

'Create something new!' was Wagner's advice, and he certainly followed this himself. These days, it is the staging of *The Ring* which is constantly being forged anew like Siegfried's sword, and many quite startling productions have offered new insights into this eternally fascinating and, in Tchaikovsky's words, 'epoch-making' work of art.

It seems to me that, if the *Ring* is to continue to make an impact on new generations of audiences, stagings require freshness, simplicity and a sense of immediacy. Audiences should be able to feel that they are involved in some way in the great drama which is going on in their presence. In 1850, Wagner wrote in a burst of idealism

> I would design and build a theatre made of wood, invite the most suitable singers, and organise everything necessary for a special event ... Then I would invite everyone interested in my works, make sure that the auditorium is filled properly, and give three performances in a week – *gratis* of course – after which the theatre would be pulled down and the whole thing would be over for good.[1]

We can be grateful that he did not go quite that far, but his comments do provide a clue as to how he regarded his works within a theatrical tradition going back to the amphitheatres of Athens, the street theatres of the Middle Ages, and Shakespeare's wooden 'O'. He wanted *The Ring* to be accessible to anyone who was interested in it, not just a wealthy or privileged section of society. He wanted a sense of festival, a celebration of life and ideas, to which ordinary men and women would come, before 'the whole thing would be over for good'.

As we look back over the war-torn twentieth century and

forward to a new millennium in which all things seem possible, we still have good reason to be amazed by *Der Ring des Nibelungen*, the fruit of one man's intellect, and a most singular work of art.

*Valhalla
as depicted in
The Prose Edda,
1760*

Notes

An Introduction to *Der Ring des Nibelungen*
1. *Zukunftmusik* (1860)
2. Franz Liszt, *Richard Wagner's Lohengrin und Tannhäuser*, (Cologne 1852)

Das Rheingold
1. Darcy, W., *Wagner's Das Rheingold*, (Oxford 1993)
2. Wagner to August Röckel, 1854.
3. *ibid.*

Die Walküre
1. This was a theme to which Wagner returned on a number of occasions in his writings, emphasising the indivisible nature of love, be it sexual or otherwise.
2. Wagner to Karl Gaillard, 1844.
3. Cosima reported that Wagner referred to the theme as 'the glorification of Brünnhilde'. Presumably, he meant this in respect of the qualities she represented. In his letter of January 1854 to Röckel, he also referred to the redemption *of* love by Brunnhilde's action at the end of *Götterdämmerung*, through which the curse on the gold is finally redeemed. Either way, it is love which remains when the old order passes away.
4. *About Conducting* (1869)

Siegfried
1. Wagner wrote this in a letter to the painter, Ernest Benedikt Kietz.
2. J. and W. Grimm and others, *German Fairy Tales*, ed. Helmut Brackert and Volkmar Sander, (Continuum, New York 1985)
3. Berlioz, H., *Treatise on Instrumentation*, rev. by R. Strauss, (New York 1948)
4. For more details of orchestras familiar to Wagner see W.O. Cord, *An Introduction to Wagner's Der Ring des Nibelungen*. Ohio University Press, 1995.
5. Cosima's Diary entry for 9 January 1873.
6. Melba, Nellie, *Melodies and Memories*, Hamish Hamilton, London, 1925. Annotated by John Cargher, 1980.

Götterdämmerung
1. Wagner to Ernst Benedikt Kietz, 1850.

Significant dates

1813   Wilhelm Richard Wagner born in Leipzig on 22 May. Father dies.

1814   Family moves to Dresden.

1821   Stepfather Ludwig Geyer dies.

1827   Returns with family to Leipzig.

1828   First composition lessons with Gottlieb Müller.

1830   Makes a piano arrangement of Beethoven's *Ninth Symphony*. Attends Thomas-Schule in Leipzig.

1831   Composition lessons with Theodor Weinlig.

1834   Finishes opera *Die Feen*.

1836   Finishes opera *Das Liebesverbot*. Marries Minna Planer.

1837   Travels to Riga and takes post as a conductor. Cosima, daughter of Fanz Liszt and Countess d'Agoult born.

1839   Loses post in Riga. Flees creditors to Russia, London and Paris.

1840   Finishes *Rienzi* in Paris. Meets Liszt for the first time.

1841   Finishes *Der fliegende Holländer*.

1842   Moves to Dresden. First performance of *Rienzi* in Dresden. Begins work on *Tannhäuser*.

1843   First performance of *Der fliegende Holländer* in Dresden. Appointed Saxon Court Conductor.

1844   Weber's remains brought from London to Dresden.

1845   Finishes *Tannhäuser*. Writes prose sketch of *Die Meistersinger von Nürnberg*. Writes prose sketch for *Lohengrin*. First performance of *Tannhäuser* in Dresden.

SIGNIFICANT DATES

1848 Mother dies.
Finishes *Lohengrin*.
Writes prose sketch for the future *Der Ring des Nibelungen*.
Writes poem of *Siegfrieds Tod*.

1849 Writes sketch for *Jesus von Nazareth*.
Actively involved in Dresden uprising.
Escapes a police warrant, to Liszt in Weimar, then Switzerland.

1850 First performance of *Lohengrin* in Weimar under Liszt.

1851 In Zurich, writes poem of *Der junge Siegfried*.

1852 Meets Otto and Mathilde Wesendonck for the first time.
Writes poem of *Die Walküre*.
Writes poem of *Das Rheingold*.

1853 Dedicates piano music to Mathilde Wesendonck.
Begins composition of *Das Rheingold*.
Meets Cosima Liszt in Paris for the first time.

1854 In Zurich, begins composition of *Die Walküre*.
Finishes *Das Rheingold*.
First ideas about *Tristan und Isolde*.

1855 Gives concerts in London.

1856 In Switzerland, finishes *Die Walküre*.
Writes prose sketch for *Die Sieger*.
Begins composition of *Siegfried*.

1857 First ideas about *Parsifal*.
Moves to the Asyl in the grounds of Villa Wesendonck, Zurich.
Breaks off work on *Siegfried* at the end of Act Two.
Begins work on *Tristan und Isolde* and the *Wesendonck Lieder*.
Hans von Bülow and Cosima married. Honeymoon with the Wagners.

1858 Minna intercepts letter from Wagner to Mathilde Wesendonck.
Minna leaves for a health cure.
Wagner travels to Venice.

1859 Returns to Lucerne.
Finishes *Tristan und Isolde*.
Travels to Paris. Minna joins him.

1860 Allowed to return to Germany, other than Saxony.

1861 Hostile reception to *Tannhäuser* in Paris.

1862 Travels to Biebrich in the Rhineland. Minna joins him, then leaves.
Full amnesty granted by the King of Saxony.

1863 Conducts in Vienna, Prague, St Petersburg and Moscow.
Vists the Bülows in Berlin. Relationship with Cosima grows.

1864 Serious financial problems.
Meets King Ludwig II of Bavaria who provides for his debts and makes available a house on Lake Starnberg.
Cosima visits. Bülow arrives later.
Wagner moves to Munich.

1865 Isolde, the first child of Wagner and Cosima born in Munich.
First performance of *Tristan* in Munich, conducted by Bülow.
Scandal over Wagner's private life and Ludwig's financial support.
Moves to Switzerland.

1866 Minna dies in Dresden.
Wagner moves into Haus Tribschen on Lake Lucerne at the King's expense. Cosima joins him.

1867 Eva, second child of Wagner and Cosima born at Tribschen.
Finishes *Die Meistersinger von Nürnberg*.

1868 First performance of *Meistersinger* in Munich, conducted by Bülow.
After returning briefly to Bülow, Cosima and children settle at Tribschen.

1869 Wagner takes up the composition of *Siegfried* after twelve years.
Siegfried, third child of Wagner and Cosima born at Tribschen.
First performance of *Das Rheingold* in Munich, against Wagner's wishes.
Begins composition of *Götterdämmerung*.

1870 First performance of *Die Walküre* in Munich, against Wagner's wishes.
Bülow and Cosima divorced.
Wagner and Cosima married.
First performance of the *Siegfried Idyll* at Tribschen.

1871 Finishes *Siegfried*.
In Bavaria, Bayreuth Council donates land for a theatre.

1872 Foundation stone for Bayreuth theatre laid.
Travels widely in search of potential artists for a festival.

1874 King Ludwig provides financial assistance for the theatre and the building of Haus Wahnfried.
Finishes *Götterdämmerung* and the whole *Ring* cycle.

1875 Extended concert tours in aid of funds.
Produces *Tannhäuser* and *Lohengrin* in Vienna.

1876 First performance of *Der Ring des Nibelungen*, conducted by Hans Richter, opens the Bayreuth Festspiele.

1877 Conducts concerts in London to raise funds.
Considers emigrating to America.

1882 Finishes *Parsifal* in Palermo.
First performance of *Parsifal* in Bayreuth, conducted by Hermann Levi.
Travels with family to Venice.

1883 Dies in Venice on 13 February.

Further Reading

This list is intended for the reader who would like to identify general material on Wagner and *The Ring* which is likely to be available in book bhops and libraries. Many of these books contain detailed bibliographies from which particular forays may be made into the enormous resources of Wagner scholarship.

****

Barth, H., Mack, D. and Voss, E. eds. *Wagner, A Documentary Study*, Thames and Hudson, 1975.
Cord, W.O., *An Introduction to Richard Wagner's Der Ring des Nibelungen*, Ohio University Press, 1995.
Culshaw, J., *Reflections on Wagner's Ring*, Secker and Warburg, 1976.
Darcy, W., *Wagner's 'Das Rheingold'*, Clarendon Press, Oxford, 1993.
Donnington, R., *Wagner's 'Ring' and its Symbols*, Faber and Faber, 1963.
Evans, M., *Wagner and Aeschylus, The Ring and the Oresteia*, Faber and Faber, 1982.
Gutman, R., *Richard Wagner, The Man, His Mind and His Music*, Secker and Warburg, 1968.
Magee, B., *Aspects of Wagner*, Oxford, 1988.
Millington, B. ed. *The Wagner Compendium*, Thames and Hudson, 1992.
Newman, E.,*The Life of Richard Wagner*, 4 Vols. London 1933-1947.
—— *Wagner as Man and Artist*, London 1914,
—— *Wagner Nights*, Putnam 1949.
Sabor, R., *The Real Wagner,* Andre Deutsch, 1987.
—— *Richard Wagner 'Der Ring des Nibelungen'* and separate volumes on each of the four dramas, Phaidon, 1997.
Spencer, S. and Millington, B., eds.and trans. *Selected Letters of Richard Wagner*, London, 1987.
Spotts, F., *Bayreuth, A History of the Wagner Festival*, Yale, 1994.
Taylor, R., *Richard Wagner, His Life, Art and Thought*, Paul Elek, London, 1979.
Wagner, Cosima: *The Diaries 1869-1883*, 2 Vols. ed. M.Gregor-Dellin and D. Mack (Munich 1976-7); Eng. trans. G. Skelton, New York 1978-80.
Wagner, Richard, *My Life*, ed. M. Gregor-Dellin (Munich) trans. A. Gray, ed. M. Whittall, Cambridge, 1983.

Index

Aeschylus, 5, 6, 11
Alberich, 12, 15, 16, 17, 23, 24, 25, 27, 28, 29, 31, 33, 49, 63, 66, 74, 79, 80, 82, 97, 98, 102, 104, 105, 109, 110, 111, 117
Appia, Adolphe, 8

Bach, Johann Sebastian, 53, 54, 55
Bakunin, Mikhail, 31
Beethoven, Ludwig van, 8, 19
Berlioz, Hector, 76
Bosch, Hieronymus, 28
Brünnhilde
  as daughter, 14, 46, 58, 61
  as lover, 16, 88, 89, 91, 101
  as Valkyrie, 48, 50, 52, 56
  as victim, 17, 110, 111, 115
  redeems love, 57, 116, 118
Buddhism, 43, 45, 117, 118
Byron, Lord, 43

Christianity, 56, 57
Communism, 42
Critics, 1, 40, 41, 42, 87, 95, 119

Das Nibelungenlied, 64
Debussy, Claude, 76
Der Freischütz, 8, 79
Der junge Siegfried, 10, 46, 63, 66
Die Meistersinger von Nürnberg, 53, 69, 94
Die Sieger, 118
Die Zauberflöte, 68, 70
Don Giovanni, 76

Donner, 13, 33, 105
Dorn, Heinrich, 9

Erda, 12, 15, 20, 21, 30, 46, 49, 84, 85, 95, 102

Fafner, 12, 13, 15, 17, 25, 26, 27, 30, 31, 39, 49, 56, 66, 69, 73, 74, 77, 79, 80, 81, 82, 84, 85, 98, 107
Fasolt, 12, 24, 26, 30, 33, 81
Freia, 12, 25, 27, 30, 41
Fricka, 12, 14, 24, 25, 26, 33, 37, 40, 47, 48, 50, 57, 105
Froh, 13, 33, 41

Gesamtkunstwerk, 28, 93
Gibichungs, 16, 102, 107, 110
Grane, 52, 87, 96, 97, 99
Greek tragedy, 5, 6
Grimms' Fairy Tales, 28, 64, 65, 68
Gunther, 16, 17, 97, 98, 99, 100, 101, 102, 104, 105, 106, 107, 108, 109, 110, 113, 114, 115
Gutrune, 16, 97, 98, 99, 100, 103, 105, 106, 107, 109, 110, 111, 113, 115

Hagen, 16, 17, 21, 24, 97, 98, 99, 100, 101, 102, 103, 104, 105, 106, 107, 108, 109, 110, 111, 112, 113, 114, 115, 116
Hanslick, Eduard, 40
Hitler, Adolf, 32

Hunding, 13, 14, 37, 38, 46, 47, 49, 50, 55, 111

Incest, 40, 41, 42

Jesus von Nazareth, 56, 118

Leitmotivs, 20, 21, 26, 94
Liszt, Franz, 3, 4, 9, 47
Loge, 12, 13, 26, 27, 28, 29, 30, 33, 34, 39, 61, 116
Lohengrin, 3, 4, 9, 51, 76

Marx, Karl, 31, 32
Melba, Nellie, 87
Mendelssohn, Felix, 60
Meyerbeer, Giacomo, 117
Mime, 12, 15, 17, 28, 63, 66, 67, 68, 69, 70, 71, 72, 73, 74, 77, 78, 79, 80, 81, 82, 83, 84, 91, 111, 114
Morality in music, 43
Mozart, Wolfgang Amadeus, 68

Nazism, 42
Nibelheim, 12, 23, 27, 28, 53, 69, 86
Nibelungs, 9, 12, 23, 28, 29, 33, 73, 105, 117
Norns, 5, 9, 16, 84, 95, 96
Notung, 13, 15, 17, 39, 68, 69, 72, 73, 74, 78, 88, 91, 102, 107, 120

Oedipus complex, 111

Paganini, Niccolo, 43
Parsifal, 42, 76, 118

Poetic Edda, 64

Rhinemaidens, 4, 5, 12, 13, 16, 17, 23, 24, 25, 26, 28, 30, 34, 80, 101, 105, 112, 113, 115, 116
Rienzi, 117
Röckel, August, 49, 119, 120

Sayn-Wittgenstein, Princess Carolyne, 47
Sayn-Wittgenstein, Princess Marie, 84
Schopenhauer, Arthur, 24, 45, 49, 113, 117
Schweitzer, Albert, 54
Shakespeare, William, 7, 44, 121
Siegfried
   as child of nature, 15, 66, 67, 70, 81, 83
   as lover, 16, 88, 89
   as victim, 16, 99, 100, 107, 114, 115
   symbolism of character, 67, 71
Siegfrieds Tod, 9, 10, 46, 63, 66
Sieglinde, 11, 13, 14, 36, 37, 38, 39, 41, 42, 45, 46, 49, 50, 55, 56, 57, 66, 72, 91, 110, 111, 113
Siegmund, 11, 13, 14, 36, 37, 38, 39, 41, 42, 45, 46, 47, 48, 49, 50, 55, 56, 57, 61, 86, 91, 102, 110, 111
Stabreim, 23
Staging *The Ring*, 6, 7, 8, 30, 61, 121
Strauss, Richard, 75
Stravinsky, Igor, 23

INDEX

Tannhäuser, 44, 59, 90
Tarnhelm, 12, 29, 30, 31, 82, 98, 99, 100, 105, 107, 114
Thidrekssaga, 79, 104
Tribschen, 47
Tristan und Isolde, 35, 39, 69, 76, 84, 94

Uhlig, Theodor, 32

Valhalla, 12, 13, 14, 17, 24, 25, 26, 33, 34, 37, 51, 86, 96, 101, 116
Valkyries, 1, 4, 5, 11, 13, 14, 16, 35, 46, 47, 49, 50, 51, 55, 56, 58, 96, 101, 110
Verdi, Giuseppe, 29
Völsungasaga, 45

Wagner, Cosima, 47, 54, 81, 90
Wagner, Richard,
 and America, 43
 and the Jews, 32, 43
 and traditional musical forms, 28, 53, 54, 55, 82, 106, 108
 approach to composition, 3, 8, 20, 21, 22, 23, 26, 36, 38, 44, 51, 57, 76, 82, 89, 90, 94, 95, 105, 119
 attitudes to love, 25, 35, 36, 37, 112, 117, 118
 on conducting, 59, 60
 on contemporary opera, 2
 on the meaning of *The Ring*, 119, 120
 orchestration, 27, 28, 68, 74, 75, 76, 77, 78, 86
 revolutionary activities, 31, 34
 texts, 23, 45
 use of repetition, 9, 10
Wagner, Wieland, 8, 61
Wanderer, 15, 64, 73, 74, 77, 79, 80, 84, 85, 86
Weber, Carl Maria von, 8, 79
Weinlig, Theodor, 53, 55
Wesendonck, Mathilde, 35, 45
Woodbird, 2, 17, 68, 82, 83, 84, 85, 112, 114
Wotan
 and power, 13, 25, 30, 34, 39, 47, 86
 as father, 14, 37, 58, 61

Wakefield Press has been publishing good Australian books for over fifty years. For a catalogue of current and forthcoming titles, or to add your name to our mailing list, send your name and address to

Wakefield Press, Box 2266, Kent Town, South Australia 5071.

TELEPHONE (08) 8362 8800 FAX (08) 8362 7592
WEB www.wakefieldpress.com.au

Wakefield Press thanks Wirra Wirra Vineyards and
Arts South Australia for their continued support.